This book must be returned on or before
the date last stamped below, unless it
is previously recalled by the Library

Fines are incurred on overdue books
(See Library Regulations)

MARKETING
CASE STUDIES

MARKETING
CASE STUDIES

Jon Sutherland
and Nigel Gross

Pitman

To the posse, particularly Tara Beckett, Alex Pantelli,
Spencer Watson, Tim Lowe, Julie Stone, Shona Rafique,
Kevin Quinn, John Salmon and Hazel Taylor.

Pitman Publishing
128 Long Acre, London WC2E 9AN

A Division of Longman Group UK Limited

© Jon Sutherland and Nigel Gross 1992

First published in Great Britain 1992

British Library Cataloguing in Publication Data
A catalogue record for this book
is available from the British Library

ISBN 0-273-03821-4

Typeset by Avocet Typesetters, Bicester, Oxon
Printed and bound in Great Britain

Contents

Introduction and guidelines for students

Each of the case studies in this book has been drawn from in-depth interviews with key marketing personnel of the organisations which form the subject of the chapter. We have highlighted their marketing successes and failures, although not in a judgmental manner.

At the end of each of the chapters, which cover different aspects of marketing, you will find a number of activities and tasks related to the organisation, its philosophy, strategies and tactics. The principal aim of these case studies and their activities is to help you relate the theory of marketing to real-life situations and to see how they are handled beyond the textbook. A list is given on page ix of the aspects of marketing covered in each chapter.

To help you further, we have covered the main theoretical points after the activities and tasks – so no peeking at them before you tackle the problems!

Guidelines to tackling cases

1 Read through the case study.
2 Then read it again to make sure you gain a thorough appreciation of the case.
3 Read through the activities and tasks at the end of the case study.
4 Read the case again in order to relate the activities and tasks to the case.
5 Think about your answers – don't jump to conclusions. In your written answers, identify the points of theory, and apply them to the task. You will be required to present your information in a variety of different, realistic business formats. Do not write an essay!

We hope that the book proves useful to you in trying to match the theory and the practice, since some marketing theory appears to be logical in the textbook but proves impossible in the real world, for example truly accurate market research!

While this book does stand alone as a series of case studies drawn from throughout the marketing world, you will find our book *Marketing in Action* very valuable for additional information and a fuller description of the marketing terms used.

Marketing encompasses much more of the business activity of an organisation than would at first appear. We hope that this point at least comes across to you.

Finally and most importantly, marketing is fun. It abounds with ideas, new concepts and radical projects. We hope you find it as interesting as we do.

JS/NG

Note Please do not contact the organisations who have contributed cases to this book. They have been kind enough to give us permission to use their cases but they would not welcome an excessive number of enquiries from students about issues raised in them. Thank you for your co-operation.

Chart of marketing theory coverage

Case study	Theory
New Force	Franchising/Licensing/Industrial marketing/Distribution
The Automobile Association	Market segmentation
The English Vineyards Association	Public relations/PR targets and tasks/PR and marketing
Dixon Miniatures	Product types/Understanding the buyer/Creating a need (proactive marketing)
Leadon Fine Arts	Price determinance/Pricing policy
Harbour Designs	Advertising agencies/Choosing an agency/Agency role and functions/Working with an agency
Ark	Social marketing/Responsibility versus profit/Non-profit-making organisations
Sunsetters	Consumer markets/Trade markets/Target marketing/Costing
Boxtree	Launching a product/Media planning
Hoseasons Holidays	The role of the marketing manager/Setting marketing objectives/Marketing mix/Market-orientated organisations
Cosmetics To Go	Product planning/Product development/Direct marketing/Mail order/Customer loyalty
Lynx	Outdoor advertising/Celebrity and personality endorsements

ACKNOWLEDGEMENTS

We would like gratefully to acknowledge and thank the following for their invaluable contributions to this book:

Phil Cunningham and Jenny Anderson of New Force
Jenny Pizer of The Automobile Association
Gary Sankey of Harbour Designs
Commander James Bond of The English Vineyards Association
Trevor Dixon of Dixon Miniatures
Don Dodds of Leadon Fine Arts
Reg Boorer of Ark
John Dunnet and Caleb Pringle of Sunsetters
Nichola Motley and Sarah Mahaffy of Boxtree
Alan Hopley of Hoseasons Holidays
Mark Constantine and Rowena Hofbauer of Cosmetics To Go
Graeme Wotherspoon of Lynx

New Force

THE DISTRIBUTION INDUSTRY . . . .

New Force is a franchised distributor of electrical components. Distributors act as middlemen between the end-user, who might want only one item, and the manufacturer, whose costs may require making a large number of the item. The distribution industry is known for its fierce competition and often very small profit margins. Therefore, in order to survive, a company has to be extremely efficient.

Distributors form a very necessary link in the chain between the manufacturer and the end-user consumer. However, since the distributor is the main point of contact between the consumer and the manufacturer's product, the manufacturer quite rightly feels the need to take some care in choosing who is distributing and selling its product. Hence the concept of franchising has become popular in the distribution field.

Most people tend to think of franchises in terms of the few well-known names, such as Kentucky Fried Chicken, Wimpy and Rentokil. However, franchising is far more widespread, and in industry it forms probably the largest sector of general marketing on behalf of manufacturers. New Force has chosen to specialise in the distribution of electrical components and has acquired a number of franchises for these products.

If a distribution company wins a franchise (how this is achieved we will discuss a little later), it will receive favourable treatment from the manufacturer, including a very favourable pricing structure that will enable it to be competitive in the marketplace.

With an arrangement like this both parties will, in theory, do well. The manufacturer has acquired a good 'front end' for its marketing policy, and the distributor has acquired favourable prices with which it can work.

THE NEW FORCE – MATSUSHITA FRANCHISE DEAL . . . .

Obtaining the franchise

For our case study we are going to look at the Matsushita franchise, which was recently acquired by New Force, a small to medium-sized distribution company servicing the electronics industry. Matsushita is a very large Japanese manufacturer of electronic components with a very competitive and desirable range of products. New Force recognised that the Matsushita line would be extremely beneficial to its own existing business and set about putting together a bid for a franchise agreement. (The bid is a set of offers describing what the distributor can do for the manufacturing company – you may remember a similar process occurring with the independent TV companies in 1991.)

The contents of an offer must be carefully considered by both parties. On the one hand, the manufacturer is looking for someone who will buy (and in turn sell) large amounts of its product with the minimum of effort on its own part. On the other hand, the distributor is looking to spend as little money as possible (keeping product in stock is an integral part of franchising and distribution, and storage is very expensive). The distributor also wants to get as much 'support' – the industry term – as possible in technical advice, marketing campaigns and cheap prices from the manufacturer. Get the offer wrong and you will either lose the bid – which is bad enough – or win the franchise and not make any money – which is even worse!

We interviewed Phil Cunningham, New Force's Managing Director, who said that the initial negotiation process was absolutely critical, and it seems that the finer points could well fill a chapter in its own right. The actual conditions agreed very much depended on the two companies involved. Here, New Force had a distinct advantage.

Matsushita had been growing, not only by traditional methods but also through the acquisition of other companies. One of these was SDS Ltd, a company whose products New Force had been selling sucessfully for some years. Obviously, this existing track record had a great influence in persuading Matsushita that New Force would indeed be able to achieve the sales figures it promised. Although the finer points of the agreement must, of course, remain confidential, we were fortunate enough to have full access to the company's marketing strategies when it came to launching and then building on its newly acquired franchise.

Making the franchise work

If New Force had been starting from scratch, there would have been a pressing need for market research. Indeed, this would normally come before a bid is even put together in order to estimate the potential revenue which could be achieved. As it was, the company already had extensive information on the potential markets – and certainly enough to know how to go about marketing its new acquisition.

New Force's basic campaign philosophy – the company uses more or less the same strategy right across the board – has two main thrusts:

1 An advertising campaign.
2 A series of contacts both via the telephone and through face-to-face meetings.

New Force has a very well-developed appreciation of advertising. Every advertisement it has ever placed has been kept on file and its relative success logged for future reference, a simple exercise but one often ignored.

The company uses two media for its advertising. The first is *Electronics Components*, a magazine serving the electronics industry. Its circulation is small, but the readershp is very highly representative of New Force's potential customers. Specific targeting is obviously very important with specialised products such as these.

ig 1
dvertorial utilising
e Matsushita name.

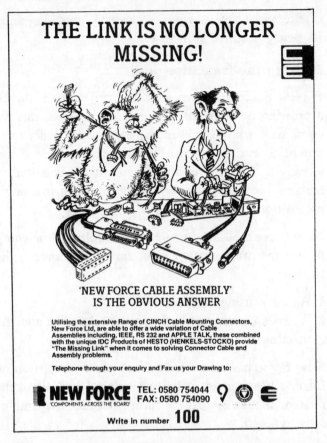

Fig 2
The humorous touch.

The second major medium is the company's catalogue. This is now produced every year and is available to all potential customers, forming a standard part of most mail-outs. New Force considers the catalogue not only as a means of allowing customers to select the products they require, but also as an active marketing tool. New franchises receive specific attention in the catalogue through advertisements as well as general product information. This feature of the campaign is used as a major selling point when tendering for the franchise in the first place. To an outsider, this may appear a simple idea but its usage is not as common as you might think.

The magazine advertising is worth looking at more closely, not only because of its specific relevance to franchises, but also for the careful way in which the campaign has evolved. We have reproduced in this chapter examples drawn from the last few years. The first thing to notice is the variation in strategies as the company explored different avenues. The results indicated that advertisements with a very specific theme – the 'Aries', for example – had a much better response rate than the more general features. The comedy approach had disappointing results, as is often the case. Lately, the company has begun to utilise the pseudo editorial – or 'advertorial' – style, and this has again proved to be relatively successful.

Each of the advertisements is specifically designed to produce enquiries for the company rather than actually sell something directly, since it is on the basis of these enquiries that the company's salesforce can get to work. Even from the advertisements for specific items, sales of a more general nature are generated. New Force's MD is convinced that responses are generated by an interest in something

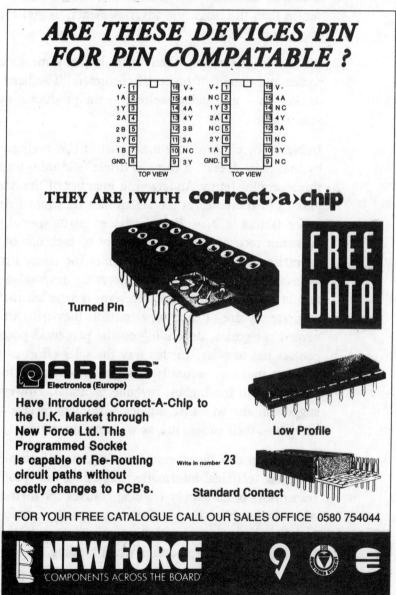

Fig 3
Concentrating on a specific product to generate enquiries – by far the most successful of the three advertising approaches for New Force.

new or innovative that potential customers might simply want to know about rather than purchase, such as the 'Aries' mentioned above. Once a contact has been made, no matter what the initial stimulus, the serious business of selling can begin.

The catalogue advertising, on the other hand, tends to follow a far more specific style. There is, of course, little or no point in a company advertising in its own brochure, so the advertisements carried are for the actual manufacturers of products that New Force is already selling. These tend to be of a more general, almost 'PR', nature than the magazine advertisements, as you can see from the example in Fig 1.

All of this advertising, then, is really just a means of obtaining the names and details of potential customers. The hard graft of marketing – and indeed selling – the product is carried out by the sales team.

In New Force's case, the main part of this marketing is carried out by the 'Sales Desk', a combined tele/field sales team consisting of three people. Jenny Anderson, a member of this team with many years' of experience in the electronics franchise field, cited one of the major factors in New Force's success as its special attention to its customer records. Every respondent to each one of the company's advertisements is contacted by one of the team. From this call is ascertained what particular products the respondent is interested in, and in what volume. Once the team is satisfied that they have an accurate picture of their new contact, they will put this into one of several categories, depending on the perceived potential sales the contact has to offer. In this way the sales effort can be directed in an efficient manner, naturally enough concentrating most effort on the contacts with the highest revenue potential. However, this is not to suggest in any way that smaller customers receive a second-rate service – their orders are as welcome as any!

Backing up this 'front end' are a number of people able to offer specialist technical information regarding new products. Indeed, franchisors often supply training courses for their approved distributors. New Force, however, actually uses its own existing technical know-how as a selling point, not only to its own customers, but also to the manufacturer when bidding for the franchise itself.

Being able to provide this know-how is a very valuable marketing tool for the distributor, and one that should not be underestimated as it enables the company to 'design product in'. Simply put, this means persuading electronics designers to insist that product 'X' is used in their new designs. Once specified in such a way, it is very difficult not to have to use that specific product, and then, of course, one has achieved a virtually captive market.

New Force is a superbly professional organisation appearing to get just about everything right. One of the most common criticisms that can be levelled at franchisees is that, although they may have done all the necessary market research into their own potential markets, they have neglected to study the actual deal with the franchisor, a shortcoming that New Force has avoided.

New Force keeps very good records of its marketing efforts, from the logged responses to its advertisement campaigns to the call diaries of its salesforce. This constitutes another major aspect of its success: its ability to follow up enquiries, check the relative turnover of various customers and respond to their ever-changing needs.

ACTIVITIES AND TASKS

1 Take a slightly more accessible industry such as the grocery trade (most people have encountered the likes of Spar and Happy Shopper) and try to put together a package of your own in order to bid for a franchise.

This is very much a group activity and we suggest that you team up in pairs with one person playing the part of a franchisor and the other playing the franchisee. The franchisor can then judge the relevant merits of each offer.

However, don't forget what was said in the study above – it is easy to win a franchise bid but perhaps not so easy to do so and make money.

This activity will require a significant amount of groundwork by the reader, but the effort should prove worth while.

2 In relation to the first activity, consider the franchise operation from the other side of the fence. In the role of the managing director of a small, successful chain of retail outlets:
   a Prepare an introductory package of material regarding the franchise.
   b Design an advertisement or campaign targeted to reach potential franchisees.

   c Develop a rationale for how you would split up the UK to offer potentially profitable geographical areas within which franchisees would operate.

   d Consider exactly what you would include in the package, e.g. vehicles, shop fittings, training.

You may choose any type of retailing outlet, but consider the fact that it must be popular enough to attract the maximum number of enquiries.

THE THEORY BEHIND IT ALL . . . .

The New Force case study highlights two major marketing considerations: first the nature, growth and potential of franchising; secondly, the peculiarities of industry-to-industry trading and marketing.

1 Franchising and licensing

Franchising is an example of a joint venture between two organisations. Broadly speaking there are two distinct types of joint venture:

   a Licensing This covers a wide range of agreements relating to the actual selling (or indeed leasing) of an expertise. Some licensing agreements include the right to produce a product under patent on behalf of the licensor (the owner of the patent) by the licensee (the nominated producer). In the case of New Force it involves the right to use a particular trademark or brand name. In return for these rights, the licensee pays an agreed sum, usually annually. In addition to this, the licensee will often pay a percentage of turnover. Remember that the licence may not necessarily involve a physical product but rather a service. In such cases it is called an 'intangible licence'.

   b Franchising This is basically a form of licensing. The franchisor provides a standard package of 'ingredients' such as shop fittings, vehicles, training programmes, management systems, etc. Alternatively, it may involve the transfer of rights to produce a product in a given geographical area. A good example of this is Coca Cola, which franchises bottling plants all over the world. Other well-known franchisors are Benetton, Kentucky Fried Chicken, Body Shop and Burger King.

2 Industrial marketing

Consider the distribution channels of industry and specifically the role of the 'middleman' or distributor. The two major concerns of any distribution channel are the accessibility and availability of a product. Middlemen are used extensively in easing these particular problems, but in order to distribute the products they will demand a cut of the profits. It would seem logical, then, that most manufacturers would choose to distribute their own products and keep that extra profit. In reality, however, the opposite is the case. Why?

These are the advantages of using middlemen:

- They can act as a warehouse for the manufacturer, buying in bulk and selling to the customer in smaller quantities.
- They can help reduce delivery times by having products in stock locally.
- They can promote the manufacturer's products at a local level.
- They can offer separate credit terms to the customer that do not affect the manufacturer's cash-flow.
- They can offer very useful after-sales service on a local basis.
- They can provide personal contact with the customer, relieving the manufacturer of this task.

Other major reasons for manufacturers setting up franchises or licensing agreements are:

- Each member of the chain helps cut costs (for many of the reasons mentioned above) and maximises profits.
- Healthy competition between outlets is encouraged, but damaging competition that wastes resources and effort should be avoided. (In many cases the exact geographical boundaries of the licence or franchise are defined.)
- Manufacturers can control the pricing structure all the way to the end-user (through profit margins and discounts).
- The manufacturer can give support to the licence-holders or franchisees by generating display materials, sales promotions and joint (or cooperative) advertising.

The Automobile Association

COMPANY PROFILE . . . .

It is probably safe to assume that every reader has heard of the Automobile Association, or AA as it is commonly known. The AA is now the largest motoring club in the UK, with more than 7.6 million members (a third of all UK motorists), and its core activity is the roadside care of motorists. It does, however, have many other strings to its bow, not least being the large Personal Lines insurance business, along with numerous other activities, from producing the radio traffic reports from AA Roadwatch to being a sizeable specialist publisher.

In this case study our main interest will be in the AA's direct marketing department, which is responsible for member services, including the recruitment and retention of members. This encompasses a wide range of activities, for instance the encouragement of members to upgrade membership cover, and we shall elaborate on these later.

The person responsible for this function is Jenny Pizer. Jenny has a staff of sixteen people, divided into four units:

1 Recruitment
2 Retention
3 Special Services
4 Development

The first of these units is responsible for gaining new business. The second is responsible for maintaining existing membership. The third is responsible for the marketing of member benefits and some new products and services, and it tends to be project-oriented. The fourth is, in fact, the statistical services department. These staff members maintain the AA's comprehensive member database and play a critical role in the direct marketing function, as we shall see.

THE MARKETING BRIEF . . . .

Rather than trace a specific example, we intend to highlight the general aspects of successful direct marketing activities. The term 'marketing' is used here rather than 'mail' intentionally, since it rapidly became evident during the interview for this case study that such campaigns have come a long way since the unsolicited mailshot.

Fig 4
The logo promotes the corporate image.

Although mailshots continue to play a major role in the AA's campaigns, several other direct marketing techniques are now also used, e.g. Press inserts, space adverts, telemarketing and member-get-member. All of Jenny's work is designed to elicit a response while building on the AA's image, i.e. each advertisement is for a specific service and includes some form of coded response mechanism (coupon, telephone number, etc) to allow a potential customer to get in contact with the Association.

As well as the more obvious advantage of directly generating customers, this method permits very accurate information to be gathered by which the relative success of each individual campaign can be measured. All responses are stored on the Association's database and then analysed by the Development unit. This permits not only the analysis of numbers but also the quality of response to be logged and stored. Consequently, each individual campaign can be studied in great detail and constant improvements can be implemented. This enables a very rapid evolution in techniques, leading to more cost-effective marketing campaigns.

The Association relies on its staff for analysis of the marketplace and ideas for new services to offer. Once a new service is identified, the usual creative process is followed to produce the actual content of the marketing campaign. This process is not one that we can cover here in any great detail and we would refer you to other case studies in this book for a fuller discussion of campaign planning. Suffice it to say that both in-house resources and external agencies are utilised in this process. After this development period, several alternative packages are produced that pass on to the next stage of field testing.

The first point of interest is that the AA steers clear of regional testing. This is a technique often used by manufacturers of FMCG (fast moving consumer goods, e.g. chocolate, soap powder) to test new products. Where TV advertising is important, regional testing makes sense since costs are greatly reduced. Such testing does, however, introduce a statistical anomaly into any results, since there are acknowledged regional differences in consumer attitudes. Even when mechanisms are introduced to combat these, the results are still open to a higher degree of error than would be the case if a truly random sample were taken from across the country.

The AA uses its database to select a random cross-section of targets. It also selects a compatible sample to act as a control for the 'experiment'. The term 'control' is one borrowed from science. Simply put, it means that 10 000 young people would receive a standard membership mailshot and another 10 000 would receive a new mailshot specifically designed to appeal to them. The response results could then be analysed to see if there is any relative advantage in using the new package. The number involved in the sample is calculated to provide a statistically accurate result, and this would be typically around the 10 000 mark.

The designs of different packages can vary a great deal but the variances are often relatively minor, perhaps as little as a subtly different opening paragraph for the written content. It is widely acknowledged that people will usually read only the first three lines of anything before getting bored. Their interest must therefore be captured immediately to make them read on.

The constant flow of data and its continual testing are crucial to the AA's marketing strategy and allow the Association to maintain its position as market leader. The AA's computer database goes considerably further than storing data. The exact details of this are not included since we have no wish to give away any 'trade secrets'.

The Association must keep in touch with its members on a yearly basis for the renewal of subscriptions. This forms the basis of a relationship marketing approach – something which is very important to the ongoing marketing strategy. This is further helped by the marketing database being also part of the Association's main computer database, which is used to maintain the AA's general information requirements regarding its members. It may seem strange that one of the few items of information not held on the database is the type of car that a member drives. This is because the Association's policy is to cover drivers for whatever vehicle they are driving rather than for a specific vehicle.

All data obtained from respondents is exhaustively analysed to try to identify the 'typical' respondent. This is related to the process of targeting an age group, but in reverse. Where a specific market is

Fig 5
Three images on loose inserts targeting different markets together with the inside of the inserts (bottom right) showing the option choices.

first identified, the computer then puts together a mailing list of suitable targets. With more general packages, the computer will analyse returns and attempt to recognise a pattern so that the new campaign can be more efficiently targeted. The process is, therefore, constantly evolving to reflect the actual marketplace.

The Data Protection Act 1984 has obviously had an impact on the AA's activities, although this seems to have meant increased administration rather than causing any actual change to the techniques that the AA employs.

In conclusion, we should point out that, despite all this data storage, analyses and administrative effort, there is still an element of chance in this type of marketing. That said, we would quote Jenny, 'Testing is the lifeblood of our business . . .'.

REVIEW . . . .

Although we were no strangers to the techniques now available to organisations with the resources to acquire and utilise them, speaking to the AA came as something of a shock. Discussing techniques in detail with the people who actually use them shows that the scale and complexity of their activities can be 'awesome', to use a buzz word.

The sheer scale of the Association's activities is difficult enough to comprehend. Actively serving 4.5 million private members, not to mention the considerable number of corporate members, is a mammoth task in its own right. The degree of control required over these marketing activities adds a whole new dimension to be considered.

The use of computer technology can only increase in such a large-scale marketing activity. This is obviously where the future lies. Before we become entranced with the technology, however, perhaps we should step back a little and consider what the AA is trying to achieve. Put simply, this is the production of good, accurately-targeted campaigns that build relationships with members. Something that is shown to be a marketing requirement throughout this book. Today's technology allows major organisations like the AA to have the advantages of the small company as well as the large, giving a rapid response to changes in market structure. Knowledge of details and the accurate manipulation of such information allows control. Give this control to talented people and you cannot help but be successful.

Our thanks to the AA and Jenny Pizer in particular for their help in compiling this study. This chapter proved to be most interesting to compile and we trust that it is equally interesting to read.

ACTIVITIES AND TASKS . . . .

1 In the light of what you have read in this case study, which do you think are the three core facets of a direct marketing campaign?

2 The Data Protection Act 1984 has increased the costs of this type of direct marketing. In view of this, do you think that the Act should be changed to exempt reputable companies like the AA?

3 There is, at the time of writing, talk of introducing European legislation to control the amount of unsolicited mail sent to private householders. Do you think that this is justified, given the volume of unsolicited mail involved, or is it an unwarranted infringement of an organisation's ability to use such marketing techniques?

4 All the advertising methods we have discussed are designed to elicit a direct response. How do you think this compares with general image-building campaigns in terms of cost-effectiveness? Is one approach better than the other, or is there room for both approaches?

5 The use of databases in marketing is very important to the AA. There are now many commercial database packages available to run on most of the popular systems, which can provide similar data storage and analysis (albeit on a reduced scale) to the features offered by the AA's computer system.

To give you an insight into the types of function carried out, tailor a database of your own to keep track of a small direct marketing operation.

There is no right or wrong way to do this, as there are many valid solutions to any given set of problems. However, the attempt will prove very useful when it comes to understanding the intricacies of modern information management.

We suggest that you limit yourself at most to 50 potential customers, as any more will prove too time-consuming.

THE THEORY BEHIND IT ALL . . . .

The accurate identification of potential markets is a critical factor in any marketing strategy. One of the most basic aspects to be considered in this area is that of market segmentation.

Generally, this is a way of classifying individuals to reflect their preferences when it comes to consuming goods and services. For example, a working-class couple from a council estate in Liverpool are, we are told, more likely to be interested in cut-price holidays to Malaga and satellite TV than a single middle-class woman living in West Sussex. The system is far from perfect, and is very open to criticisms from certain quarters as regards its rather stereotypical view of the public. For all that, it does provide a good deal of information, and is to a greater or lesser degree utilised by nearly all marketing agencies.

There are many variations of the basic concept developed to suit a particular need. The basic segmentation criterion from which these have grown are as follows:

1 Age
2 Sex

3 Family size and life cycle
4 Social class
5 Neighbourhood
6 Education.

1 Age

The age of a consumer strongly affects the types of product they are likely to buy. With the young under 21 age group there is a strong slewing towards products that are instantly gratifying . . . fashion, fast food, alcohol and a shying away from goods such as insurance, household consumables and the like.

Age is one of the major considerations in any segmentation analysis and, whatever exceptions you may think of, the above generally holds true.

2 Sex

Like age, sex is a basic and important criterion. In many instances the effects of sex are very straightforward . . . there is little or no point in attempting to sell women's hosiery to a male market.

However, there are also many more subtle variables, mainly in the way that the two sexes react to different marketing techniques. There is no doubt that both men and women drivers have a need for the AA's services. Their reaction to marketing strategies is, however, very different. A man might, for instance, react favourably to a campaign that suggested being in the AA would make him irresistible to women. It goes without saying that most women's reactions to the same campaign would not be so favourable.

3 Family size and life cycle

There are eight recognised stages in a person's life:

a Young and single
b Young couple with no children
c Young couple, youngest child under six
d Young couple, youngest child over six
e Older couple with children 18+ living at home
f Older couple with no children living at home
g Older and single.

The ways in which these structures are utilised by the marketeer are numerous and often complex. Some of the more obvious ones would be the marketing of baby products (little use to anyone except category c), expensive luxury goods (unlikely to appeal to category c due to finances) and so on.

4 Social class

In reality this is a mix of both social class and income. The scale is divided into six main categories:

A   Higher managerial, administrative and professional
B   Intermediate managerial, administrative and professional
C1 Supervisory, clerical, junior administrative or professional
C2 Skilled manual workers
D   Semi-skilled manual workers
E   State pensioners, widows, casual and lowest grade earners.

Although this method of segmentation is the one that comes in for the most scathing of criticisms it is still nevertheless very useful. We also feel that some of the criticisms are due more to political dogma than logical objection.

5 Neighbourhood

This is one of the newest of the segmentation criteria and is defined by the initials ACORN (A Classification Of Residential Neighbourhoods). It is far too complex to discuss in any detail here but basically uses the type of dwelling in which someone lives as a defining criterion, i.e. those living in a big house in the country are more likely to buy a Rolls Royce that those in the above-mentioned council house in Liverpool.

For more information on this topic we would draw your attention to pp. 28 and 29 in *Marketing in Action*, the companion volume to this book.

6 Education

This is perhaps the least useful classification in this day and age. It relies on the old adage that better educated people drink wine and read *The Guardian*, and people who went to a comprehensive school drink lager and read the *Sunday Sport*. Both of the authors ruin this classification by doing all four! Seriously though, this is obviously a gross generalisation even by the standards of other segmentation criteria and is being used less and less.

The information acquired from this type of analysis is open to much interpretation, and it is perhaps in this interpretation that the true skill of targeting lies. It is very easy to poke holes in the criteria; however, anyone doing so should bear in mind that in terms of generality they remain a reasonably accurate way of segmenting markets.

The English Vineyards Association

The wine industry in Britain is still very much in its infancy, and has a great deal of work to do to achieve any degree of recognition when competing with the gigantic and well-respected European producers. This task is made even more difficult when one considers the scorn with which most (ill-informed) people view the product.

To overcome this problem the fledgling industry has formed the English Vineyards Association. The association has many tasks like most trade associations, but one of its most important is the general promotion of the product both domestically and abroad.

Before proceeding further we must make the point that we are talking here of 'English' wines, i.e. those made from home-produced grapes, and not 'British' wines which, although made in this country, often contain grapes grown abroad and are generally of a far inferior quality to their 'English' counterparts.

THE HISTORICAL CONTEXT . . . .

Commercial wine production was started in England just after the Second World War by a few wine enthusiasts. Since then the industry has grown steadily, reaching a peak of production in 1983 when approximately 3.3 million bottles were produced. In the following years the number dipped dramatically due to inclement weather conditions, but by 1990 it had climbed back to over 3 million once more.

The Association itself was founded in 1967 and, although its formation was very much a team effort, the prime mover behind it all was one of the early English wine growers and promoters, Mr Jack Ward. The Association originally had only 16 full members (actual wine producers) and 50 or so associate members (people with some other interest in the industry). Today the membership has grown to 440 full members and a considerably larger number of associate members.

The Association's early years were mostly spent in getting the industry up and running, rather than in any true form of public relations or marketing as we would understand the term today. There was much lobbying of the government to treat the industry as it would other types of agriculture as regards subsidies and so on, and to reduce the amount of duty levied on wine for domestic consumption, a theme which continues to this day.

The Association's first professional efforts started in the early 1980s and coincided fortuitously with the boom in consumption of wine in the UK.

The present head of the Association, Commander James Bond perceived three main problems that the Association had to address:

1 The perceived cost of a bottle of English wine appeared high.
2 Media coverage tended to be scornful of the product, despite its quality.
3 There were no recognised methods of 'grading' the wine as there were abroad. European countries have a number of divisions of wine – Vin de Table, Appellation Contrôlée, Qualitätswein mit Prädikat, and so on.

The first problem is one already mentioned, the amount of duty levied by the government, and is one yet to be solved. The problem is bound up with EC regulations and the government's general indifference towards the industry. Extensive lobbying continues in an effort to rectify the problem and, although important to the Association's broad purpose, it really falls outside the scope of this book.

A PERSONAL MARKETING STRATEGY . . . .

The second problem has proved to be the one to consume most of the Association's efforts. Even today the average wine drinker probably perceives English wine as a bit of a joke. In the early 1980s it was even worse, with serious wine writers rubbishing the product without bothering even to taste it!

The Association set about remedying this. We must point out here that the Association has a tiny budget of considerably less than £100 000 per year to run its entire operation, so obviously any high-profile and expensive activities would be quite out of the question.

Professional skill had to take over, and here the Association had a considerable advantage in Commander Bond, for although he would never claim to be a skilled PR man in the classical sense of the word (indeed he had no training and very little experience before taking the position), he has the one thing all good PR people need, charisma.

Now, as the scope of activities open to the Association were limited by the funds available, national press campaigns were out of the question. However, Commander Bond set about getting press coverage without paying for it, and it is here that the all-important charisma came into play. Gaining press coverage is a very difficult thing to do, especially when a sustained campaign of beneficial PR is required. Getting it when the product to be promoted is regarded with such derision makes the task almost Herculean.

Rather than batter his head against the proverbial brick wall, Commander Bond looked at the problem laterally and set about getting himself into the press 'somehow', aiming to slip in a plug for the product as an aside. Commander Bond now brought into play his 'secret weapon', so to speak. Obviously, anyone with the name Bond is going to be of passing interest, and when that person also happens to be a former Commander in the Royal Navy as well, then the novelty value will often get some media coverage.

To date this tactic has been very successful. We were shown a pile of magazines and newspapers some two feet thick containing coverage for Commander Bond and the Association, varying from simple pieces on the 'real James Bond' to articles on food and, not surprisingly, wine.

This process of personality projection as a means to getting the Association's point across has extended to other fields as well. He is often a guest speaker at various functions across the country, and although many of these are wine associations, there is a significant number of other functions of a more general interest.

Not slow to spot a new opportunity, the Association now also provides wine tastings as an adjunct to corporate hospitality. These have proved to be very successful and not only give another opportunity to extol the virtues of the English wine industry but also a valuable source of additional revenue. These events, although arranged by the Association, are actually carried out by some of the vineyards themselves.

The Grape Press

79th Edition July 1991

English Vineyards Association

**Fig 6
The Association's
booklet.**

One further thing that the Association does, unlike many other PR agencies, is to monitor carefully what is being written about it and approach media organisations which it feels are treating it unfairly in order to gain a right of reply. This is again a successful tactic and one that also contributes to the Association's wide media coverage. Finally, the Association publishes a journal (see Fig 6). This is directed at the person already interested in the product to keep them abreast of all the latest news and developments.

All of the above functions are carried out on behalf of the industry in general with no favouritism shown to any particular 'brand'. As part of the Association's rules, such functions are not allowed to actually 'market' the product, the activities being strictly limited to a true PR role.

CLASSIFICATION . . . .

The third of our points above, the question of grading, may at first sight appear relatively trivial. However, because of the myriad rules and regulations imposed by the EC, it has become one of the major thrusts of the Association's activities.

When the wine industry was formed in this country, the EC never really expected it to be anything more than a cottage industry, and probably an unsuccessful one at that. As such, no allowances were

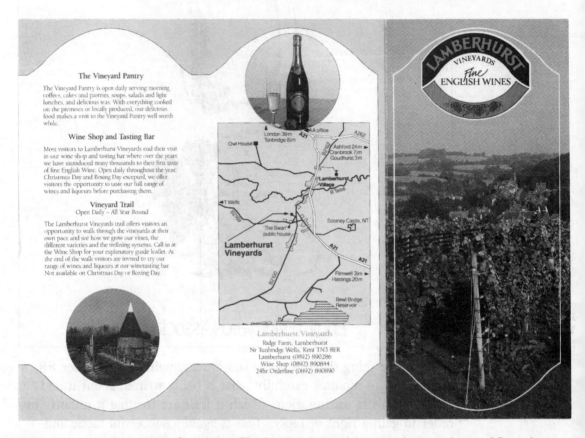

**Fig 7
A typical brochure showing the kind of promotion and marketing for vineyards which the Association seeks to encourage.**

made for giving England any status as a wine producer. Now that production is counted in the millions of bottles the EC has 'capped' production at its present output. Obviously, this is of the greatest concern to the English producers and something which the Association has been lobbying heavily to rectify for some time. Things move slowly and a result is yet to be achieved.

In the meantime the English wine industry has no way of grading its wine, which leaves the general public with no idea of which wine is regarded highly and which is not (unless they happen to be experts).

To this end the Association has recently introduced a series of medals – bronze, silver and gold – to be awarded to wines of particular merit. The handing out of these awards is strictly controlled by the Association, and the provision of the associated labels to be applied to the recipients' bottles is likewise very closely monitored.

In the summer of 1991 when we conducted the interview, this scheme was just starting and the first delivery of stickers had just been received. Consequently, it was impossible to judge if the scheme would have the desired effect. Unfortunately, without it, and if lobbying the EC fails, all English wine is doomed to be classified as 'table wine'.

In conclusion, it must be said that the English Vineyards Association achieves remarkable success, when one considers the minuscule budget with which it has to work, and is a glowing example of what can be done without spending a fortune. But – and this is a big 'but' – we must point out the dangers of a PR campaign that relies so heavily on a charismatic individual, which Commander Bond undoubtedly is. Everything runs well as long as that person remains in his or her position. Should they leave, however, the organisation instantly loses its main marketing tool.

We hope that this does not befall the Association, and it would seem that their cause is now well enough established in its own right for this not to happen.

ACTIVITIES AND TASKS

1 Assuming that, instead of having the personality of Commander Bond, you had a budget of £1 million to promote English wine. How would you plan the campaign?

2 Put yourself into the shoes of a PR agency trying to get coverage for a new range of sports shoes but with no budget. What story or angle would you use to get yourself heard?

3 We have touched on the complexities of problems facing the English wine grower when it comes to EC regulations. Research these further – the information will be readily available at larger reference libraries and indeed the DTI. Then prepare a full list of all the regulations you feel might cause a problem and details of how you would overcome them.

4 If the Association is successful in getting the wine production quota for the UK raised, how best do you think they can fully exploit the potential market, i.e. should they go for the mass market end, or concentrate as they are at the moment on the slightly more expensive middle band?

THE THEORY BEHIND IT ALL . . . .

This case study offers us the opportunity to look in depth at public relations. Let's start with a definition of PR, the arm of a company's marketing strategy which seeks to project a generally favourable image of the company, its public face if you like.

PR targets

There are a number of target groups that a PR exercise must aim for:

- the general public
- the company's workforce
- financial institutions
- the company's customers
- the media.

PR tasks

Having defined PR generally, now let's refine that with some more detail:

- To identify specific groups (e.g. investors, pressure groups, etc.) and then attempt to influence their thinking towards the company.
- To offer counselling and advice to various departments within a company regarding any 'outside' attitudes that could influence the company (this also includes forward forecasting of developments).
- To support and augment the company's more general marketing thrust.
- To create a 'good feeling' towards the company in the media, and wherever possible to gain coverage that portrays the company in a favourable light.
- To promote unity and a positive attitude amongst larger companies' various divisions (particularly in multinationals).
- To lobby both the government and other legislators into making decisions favourable to the company.

PR in the marketing context

Public relations and marketing are obviously two closely related disciplines. Specifically PR can contribute:

- To product publicity.
- To informing the marketplace of any new developments.
- To coordinating the advertising and sales promotions with its own more general PR strategy.
- By creating a positive and favourable image of the company, therefore increasing the effectiveness of the marketing campaign.

Dixon Miniatures

Many readers may not have heard of the wargames' market. Nevertheless it is a massive business that caters for over 100 000 regular wargamers in the UK alone, and has an estimated combined turnover of £24 million (a conservative figure).

So what is wargaming? Basically, the cynics would call it 'playing with toy soldiers'. The committed wargamer, on the other hand, would call it 'a social tabletop game with metal miniatures'.

Trevor Dixon established Dixon Miniatures in January 1976. Previously, he had gained valuable experience working for one of the (then) leading manufacturers Hinchliffe, where he worked as a mould-maker and caster.

Trevor started as a one-man business, initially making larger-scale models. They were not very successful – Trevor admits 'they weren't up to much, in hindsight'. In late 1976, he moved into the wargames' market with a range of Steppes nomads and Mongols.

By 1977, he had released the first of his samurai (Japanese warriors), and diversified into the medieval and renaissance periods soon afterwards. He decided that the best plan was to experiment with different periods and see what took off.

Fig 8 (opposite) A catalogue page of Wargaming figurines, showing that it is possible to give a quality image on a low budget.

Trevor designs his own figures, although lately he has been employing a freelance designer. He is basically responsible for everything that the company undertakes. He employs three full-time workers who do everything from casting the figures in the centrifuge to making model moulds and packing orders. His wife also helps out with paperwork and bookkeeping.

KNOWING WHAT TO MAKE AND SELL . . . .

Trevor likes to create a new range of figures to exploit an, as yet, untapped market. He says, 'you get a nose for what will go.' In other words, if you know the market, then you can try to predict

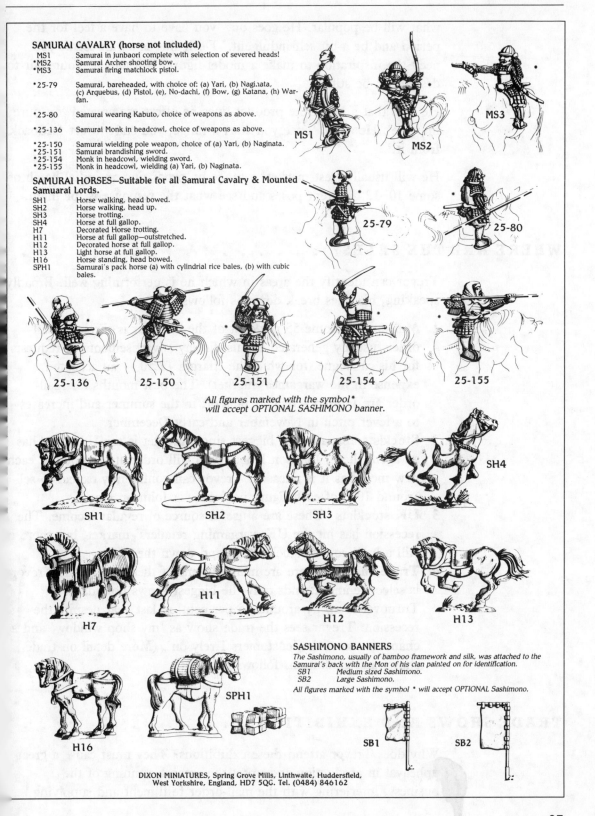

SAMURAI CAVALRY (horse not included)

MS1	Samurai in junbaori complete with selection of severed heads!
*MS2	Samurai Archer shooting bow.
*MS3	Samurai firing matchlock pistol.
*25-79	Samurai, bareheaded, with choice of: (a) Yari, (b) Naginata, (c) Arquebus, (d) Pistol, (e) No-dachi, (f) Bow, (g) Katana, (h) War-fan.
*25-80	Samurai wearing Kabuto, choice of weapons as above.
*25-136	Samurai Monk in headcowl, choice of weapons as above.
*25-150	Samurai wielding pole weapon, choice of (a) Yari, (b) Naginata.
*25-151	Samurai brandishing sword.
*25-154	Monk in headcowl, wielding sword.
*25-155	Monk in headcowl, wielding (a) Yari, (b) Naginata.

SAMURAI HORSES—Suitable for all Samurai Cavalry & Mounted Samurai Lords.

SH1	Horse walking, head bowed.
SH2	Horse walking, head up.
SH3	Horse trotting.
SH4	Horse at full gallop.
H7	Decorated Horse trotting.
H11	Horse at full gallop—outstretched.
H12	Decorated horse at full gallop.
H13	Light horse at full gallop.
H16	Horse standing, head bowed.
SPH1	Samurai's pack horse (a) with cylindrial rice bales, (b) with cubic bales.

*All figures marked with the symbol**
will accept OPTIONAL SASHIMONO banner.

SASHIMONO BANNERS

The Sashimono, usually of bamboo framework and silk, was attached to the Samurai's back with the Mon of his clan painted on for identification.

SB1	Medium sized Sashimono.
SB2	Large Sashimono.

*All figures marked with the symbol * will accept OPTIONAL Sashimono.*

DIXON MINIATURES, Spring Grove Mills, Linthwaite, Huddersfield, West Yorkshire, England, HD7 5QG. Tel. (0484) 846162 what will be popular. He goes on, 'you have to have a feel for the period and be a bit self-indulgent.' Designing is an art-form, you need the inspiration to make a model figure. Without it, your flair to design can be stifled.

He says that a lot of the product lines he offers are created 'on pure impulse'. He adds, 'once you start a range, you start to get feedback from it.'

He will usually 'test market' a range by producing an initial batch of some 10–12 different poses and see what the response is for them.

WHERE ARE THE SALES? . . . .

Trevor can identify the areas in which he is performing well. Broadly speaking, his sales break down as follows:

1 **Mail-order** Some 55 per cent of the business is through mail-order, usually generated by his display advertisements or requests for his catalogue (for which he charges £2.50 – an accepted expense in the wargames' market). The best months for mail-order are January–May. It tails off in the summer and increases to a fever pitch in November and early December.
2 **Stockists abroad** His biggest single market is the USA. He has an agent there, Johnson Hood, who will order at least 500 of each new model as it is released. Trevor can confidently expect to sell around 1000 of each figure per year via Johnson Hood.
3 **UK stockists** These are a useful source of regular income. The recession has hit the UK wargaming retailers' market, but there is still a hard-core of stockists up and down the country.
4 **Trade shows** There are many dozens of these each year. Trevor is selective and attends only the biggest shows nowadays. Turnover is up by around 25 per cent on last year despite the recession. Trevor sees the trade show as 'my shop window' and a chance to meet the 'customers I rely on'. (More detail on trade shows and exhibitions follows below.)

TRADE SHOWS AND EXHIBITIONS . . . .

Why does Trevor attend these exhibitions? They must cause a great upheaval in production and upset the smooth running of the business, interfering with the mail-order fulfilment and supplying stockists. However, he is certain that they are worth doing, as not only do they bring in much needed instant cash, but, he maintains, 'everybody throughout the country has easy access.'

Trevor now attends some five shows a year, covering the entire country well:

1 Colours – at Reading
2 Salute – in London (where sales were up 25–30 per cent this year)
3 The World Championships – at Derby
4 Claymore – in Edinburgh
5 The Triples – in Sheffield

Elsewhere he is represented by stockists who have agreed to attend those shows he does not. Principally these representatives are Paul and Theresa Bailey, based in the West Country.

STOCK CONTROL AND ORDER FULFILMENT

Trevor maintains a basic stock of all of his figure range. He recognises the investment in metal and casting time, but knows that this is really the only way of being able to turn orders around quickly.

He has just invested around £700 on a new racking system that makes the job of collecting the models for an order a lot easier. Dixon Miniatures occupies the top floor of a mill, and has around 3000 square feet of floor space. The work can be labour intensive, since each mould carries only some twenty models, and big orders take a long time to be fulfilled if there is no stock ready. In any event, he aims to turn a mail-order around in under three weeks on average.

COMPETITION AND PRICE

His main competitors are Wargames Foundry, a Nottingham-based firm which is an offshoot of Games Workshop. Competition is an ever-present problem. Trevor says: 'It was easier in the early days, but now there's very little that isn't done by someone else. You either have to get there first, or be better if they're there already.'

As to price, we asked if the market was price sensitive. 'Yes, to a

25mm READY MADE ARMIES

To save you the work of having to sit down and work out the number and type of figure you need to compile your wargame armies, DIXON MINIATURES have compiled the most suitable figures from our most popular 25mm ranges to create as near as possible a typical army of the period. Each army comes to you in a classical black presentation box (approx. 12" x 9" x 1½) with inner dividers. All you do is choose your army from the list below.

Also you will note from the prices quoted, that our army packs work out over 10% cheaper in some cases than buying the figures individually.

SAMURAI ARMIES

Including all seperate weapons (where appropriate) and horses for cavalry.

SAM/AP1 EARLY SAMURAI – 12th - 16th c

Contains:
33 Cavalry (inc. 3 standards)
100 Samurai Infantry
60 Peasants

SAM/AP2 LATE SAMURAI – c 1550 - 1615

Contains:
2 Mounted Generals
10 Cavalry
20 Samurai foot
144 Ashigaru (inc. Standards)
10 Peasants
107 Sashimono banner

SAM/AP3 SAMURAI IKKO'IKKI MONK ARMY – c 16th c

Contains:
1 Mounted General
8 Cavalry
120 Samurai foot (inc. 3 standards)
80 Sashimono banner

GA/AP1 GRAND ALLIANCE OR LATE 17th Century European

(Allmounted figures include horses)

Contains:
1 Mounted General
3 Mounted Officers
23 Cavalry
96 Infantry
2 6pdr gun and crew
1 Pioneer group

GA/AP2 LOUIS XIV ARMY - Late 17th - early 18th Century

Contains:
As above but different Infantry and some Cavalry
(Ask for details if required)

FRENCH IN EGYPT – 1798 - 1801

NAP/AP1(a) FRENCH ARMY – 1798 - 1801

Infantry dressed in Bicorn and Long Tailed Coat, Cavalry in Mirliton type Shako.
(All Cavalry include horses).

Contains:
1 Napoleon
1 Staff Officer
3 Mounted Officers
24 Cavalry
90 Infantry (inc. Officers and standard bearers)
4 Camels with riders
2 6" Howitzers with crew

NAP/AP1(b) FRENCH ARMY – c 1798 - 1802

Suitable for the Egypt campaign.
Infantry in Casquette and Pouf hat and Kleber ordinance tunic. Cavalry in Mirliton type shako.
Contents as NAP/AP1(a) except for dress of infantry as listed above.

25mm ARMY PACKS AVAILABLE BY MAIL ORDER ONLY

AMERICAN CIVIL WAR ARMIES

(All cavalry including horses)

ACW/AP1 – UNION ARMY

Contains:
1 Mounted General
1 General on foot
24 Cavalry (inc. Officers and Guidon bearers)
90 Infantry (inc. Officers and standards)
1 Gun, limber and six horse team
2 extra guns
12 Artillery crew

ACW/AP2 – CONFEDERATE ARMY

Contents as ACW/AP1, except figures more suitable to be used
as Confederate types. Again, ask for details if required.

PRICES:-

SAM/AP1 - SAM/AP2 – £100 each

SAM/AP3 – £75

GA/AP1 - GA/AP2 – £75 each

NAP/AP1a, b, c – £85 each

ACW/AP1 - ACW/AP2 – £85 each

POST & PACKING

UK & BFPO
Orders under £20 ADD 10% (Minimum 50p)
Orders over £20 ADD 5%
Orders over £50 POST FREE

EUROPE
Orders under £50 ADD 25% (Minimum £1)
Orders over £50 ADD 15%

OUTSIDE EUROPE & WORLDWIDE
SURFACE
Orders under £50 ADD 25% (Minimum £1)
Orders over £50 ADD 20%

AIRMAIL
Orders under £10 ADD 75% (Minimum £3)
Orders over £10 ADD 50%

DIXON Miniatures, Spring Grove Mills, Linthwaite, Huddersfield, W. Yorks, HD7 5QG. Tel: 0484 846162

Fig 9 (opposite)
This catalogue shows
the wide range of
products available and
the method of giving
price information –
note the amounts
which collectors are
prepared to pay.

large extent,' he replied. Prices have doubled in the last five years, but Dixon's policy is to keep prices stable and only increase them every two years.

Since it can take up to two days to design each figure, Trevor thinks that the 45p price tag per casting is not too much to ask. The average price from the competitors ranges from 34p to 55p. Trevor is thus somewhere in the middle.

THE FUTURE AND THE TURKEYS . . . .

Trevor has had a mixed success with certain ranges of figures. His less successful have been his Alamo range, which are 'ticking over', and his French In Egypt which are doing 'not as well as I thought they might.'

As to the future, he plans to expand further the American Civil War range, which are the market leaders in the world, and release Second World War tanks and other vehicles to back up his existing range of soldiers for the period.

ACTIVITIES AND TASKS . . . .

1 In the role of Trevor consider the possibility of supplying model soldiers to markets and outlets other than the ones he already supplies. Draw up a list of possible targets and how they could be sold through these.

2 The wargames' market is a specialist one. In the role of a venture capitalist, what would you need to know about a specialist market before considering investment?

3 Trevor has become a very successful niche marketeer. How advisable do you think it would be for him to decide to expand into a more mainstream market, such as ornamental figures to supply to jewellers' stores. What new problems would he encounter and how would he have to alter his existing marketing strategy?

THE THEORY BEHIND IT ALL . . . .

Trevor is fully conversant with the nature of his market. Many companies seem to blunder blindly into markets that they do not completely understand, but there are a few theoretical rules to help a company define its market.

Types of product

There are essentially only three different types of product:

1 **Non-durable** This is the most common type of purchase and includes those that need to be replaced on a regular basis, e.g. food.
2 **Durable** These are goods that by definition have a lengthy lifespan, e.g. electrical goods.
3 **Services** These are tasks carried out on behalf of the customer, such as education, transport and advice.

As well as these product definitions, there are also three distinct ways in which goods are actually purchased:

1 **Convenience goods** These are often bought on a regular basis and purchased with little thought, e.g. food and cigarettes. These items are usually low in price.
2 **Considered purchases** A little more thought goes into the purchase of these items, e.g. clothes, holidays, etc.
3 **Special purchases** These items require a great deal of thought and effort on behalf of the purchaser. The purchases tend to be rare and the obvious example is a house. Some of Dixon's customers would require this degree of knowledge before making a purchase.

Understanding the purchaser

1 **Who buys the product?** Understanding the 'typical' customer allows a company to aim its marketing efforts accurately at the most fruitful targets.
2 **What do they buy at present?** Having identified your customer find out what he or she is buying at the moment, i.e. research your competition.
3 **Where do they buy their product?** Further definition of a company's competition and where to find the best potential outlets for your own product.

4 **How often do they buy?** Is the product purchased daily, monthly, yearly? Are the purchases made on a regular basis or randomly?

5 **How loyal is the customer to a particular brand?** This is critically important when a company is thinking of launching a new product in direct competition with one already in the marketplace.

Creating a need (proactive marketing)

This type of marketing strategy is particularly pertinent to our case study.

Here a company attempts to manufacture a market for a new product where none previously existed. This is a very risky strategy to adopt and one that requires an extensive knowledge of the marketplace (as defined above). As well as this, a healthy degree of intuition would also prove very useful.

The credit card, such as Barclaycard or Access, would be one of the best examples of this strategy and graphically illustrates the degree of success that can be gained by being the first to bring a new product to the marketplace.

However, for every glowing success there are a considerable number of failures, whose names do not so readily spring to mind. If they did they would probably have not been failures!

Dixon has been very successful in using this approach, again illustrating how important it is to understand fully your marketplace.

CASE STUDY 5

Leadon Fine Arts

Leadon Fine Arts is a company specialising in the sale of mid-priced paintings and antiques direct to the public. These range in price from around £30 up to several thousand, although a price of around £100 would be typical.

The company, jointly run by Mr Don Dodds and his wife, was originally started back in the late 1960s more as a hobby than anything else, on a budget of £50 – even then a very small budget for a start-up!

Don and his wife had long been interested in antiques, Don simply as a collector, and his wife since she had for some years worked at Sotheby's, the famous auction house. For their own interest they had been attending antique fairs for a number of months when there was a coincidence of events that was to lead to the founding of the company.

First, they had developed an interest in buying and then reselling, and secondly a small amount of money (the £50 mentioned above) had been made available through the will of a relative.

Using at first intuition (mixed with a liberal amount of skill we suspect, even at this early time) they set about buying up 'bits and bobs' (their words not ours). This catch-all phrase meant items of small value, something they could perhaps buy for £2 and sell for £5 (at 1968 prices).

So having secured their source of supply a viable outlet was then required. In the first instance this was to be a bric-à-brac stall in Greenwich Market. This was a popular weekend market with a reputation for 'interesting junk', again the company's phrase not ours, but one which we feel is applicable in this case. The market, incidentally, is still flourishing and apparently retains much the same character as it did then.

Working first on a Saturday and then on Sunday, the enterprise prospered, with the company carrying around £300 worth of stock at any one time (again at 1968 prices).

A CHANGE IN THE MARKET . . . .

Up until that point there had been no real marketing involved in the enterprise other than correctly identifying the type of environment in which to sell their product. After a year or so, it began to become apparent that, whilst the couple had obviously got it right in as much as they were selling items and making a profit, the profit available was limited by their choice of items to sell. Until then they had concentrated on cheap items that might have high margins in percentage terms but would never provide profit of more than around £10 per item. The decision to operate at this end of the market when starting the business had been a sound one, both in the cost of start-up and the ease of marketing – such cheap items are usually (though not invariably) easier to buy and sell than expensive ones. At this point, however, the company not only had sufficient funds to move upmarket a little, they also felt they had the expertise to take the risk as well.

Although we said above that little marketing was involved in this early stage of the company, this is perhaps not strictly true since the one thing they did do was to study the market closely. At every market session one or other of the couple would always take time to wander around similar stalls in the market to see what was selling well. This may seem a simple enough thing to do, something most people would regard as common sense, but nevertheless it is a critical part of market research – know your market and you have a good chance of being successful.

So, now that the time had come to move up to items costing £50–100, the company already had a very good idea of what it was looking for, a good position to be in considering that those prices translate to £500 to £1000 in today's prices.

Sales results with their new products were not, however, as good as might have been expected. This was for one simple reason (simple at least when armed with that most wonderful of tools, hindsight): since they had changed product it therefore followed that the potential market for that product had changed as well. People with that amount of money did not tend to frequent Greenwich Market in any great numbers. As a consequence a new stall was taken in a location closer to the city (London) centre that had a reputation for more upmarket dealers.

Locating in an area already occupied by similar traders is a very common activity amongst those who specialise. Although it could be argued that there is a larger amount of competition than would otherwise be the case, it is also true that locating with similar businesses increases the supply of suitable customers. It is far more likely for an interested customer to visit an area with a dozen or so interesting shops than it is for such a customer to visit an area with only a single shop.

To supplement the marketplace provided by the new stall the company (which as previously mentioned had been attending antique fairs for some time as buyers) began to attend the occasional traders' fair.

This general type of trading continued until the late 1970s. In the meantime the company had begun to develop a speciality in pictures, mainly because it was the area of the business that interested them most rather than for any commercial considerations.

GOING INTO PICTURES . . . .

The market in pictures is very complex and one very prone to fashion. (Witness for instance the craze for Impressionists at the end of the 1980s that saw pictures changing hands for over twenty million pounds!) Leadon steered well clear of this market simply because of lack of funds! Instead they tended to deal in items valued up to several hundred pounds and ones that could be bought purely on merit rather than because of any attributable artist. Many of the pictures were bought in a rather tatty condition but were renovated and then resold. This type of activity allowed a process of 'added value' to be utilised with the works and often yielded very high margins.

By 1984 the company had acquired enough capital to expand laterally by purchasing their own renovating business. In fact it was the one they had been using for some time that came on the market at a fortuitous time. With this acquisition the business grew at a considerable pace and in 1987 Leadon held their first exhibition, the first of many which were eventually to provide their major marketing outlet. The idea was lifted from a similar event that Mr Dodds had attended himself, demonstrating that copying other people's ideas is a perfectly valid marketing tool.

The organisation of these events required a lot of planning and not inconsiderable expense. To start with a suitable venue had to be found. The area was important, since it was absolutely imperative for there to be a large supply of potential clients as the events were to last only two days (Saturday and Sunday). Such clients were best to be found in areas of reasonable affluence, and although the company experimented with various locations they settled on a small to medium-sized village hall a few miles from a major town.

The events were extensively advertised in the local press to attract attention, and Don, who is quite a flamboyant character, was never slow in obtaining media coverage whenever the opportunity arose.

LEADON FINE ARTS

Established since 1970 *Reading (0734) 64999*

On behalf of clients and collectors in the UK and overseas we urgently need to purchase collections or individual items of the following:

SILVER

ANTIQUE FURNITURE

JEWELLERY and WATCHES

WATERCOLOURS, OILS or PRINTS,

SKETCH BOOKS
(Pencil Drawings or Watercolours)

OBJETS D'ART

PORCELAIN

Please telephone to discuss an appointment with
Mr Dodds.

24 hr Answer Service: READING (0734) 64999

We also offer a prompt service for probate and clearance of effects. Executors and solicitors are invited to call in confidence – utmost discretion assured.

Fig 10
A general-purpose mailer and handout to potential sellers, buying being as important as selling to the fine art trader.

WILLIAM LIONEL WYLLIE, RA RI
1851 (London) – 1931 (London)

The half-brother of L P Smythe (qv) and the brother of C W Wyllie (qv), he was a marine painter who began to sketch as a boy at Wimereux on the French coast. He studied at Heatherley's and the RA Schools and was awarded the Turner Gold Medal 1869.

He studied the history and method of shipbuilding to help him with his paintings. At seventeen he exhibited for the first time at the Academy, and he was elected ARA and RA in 1889 and 1907. He was also a member of RI. In his twenties he worked as a maritime illustrator for the 'Graphic'. He painted historical naval subjects, the life of the Thames and docks, the contemporary Navy and yachting and dinghy sailing.

He was primarily a watercolourist, being able to sketch under the most difficult conditions, but he also painted in oil, was an accomplished etcher, and he illustrated a number of books.

He was the father of Lt. Col. HAROLD WILLIAM WYLLIE (1880-1973), also a marine painter.

His work has been exhibited at the following :

        British Museum
        Bridport Art Gallery
        Brighton Art Gallery
        Towner Gallery, Eastbourne
        Fitzwilliam
        Glasgow Art Gallery
        Greenwich
        Maidstone Museum
        City Art Gallery, Manchester

    ETCHING :   Racing Yachts in the Solent

Fig 11
An example of the extra information Leadon provides to assist in the marketing of its paintings – their experience has shown that the artist's history adds to the value of the work.

The events were an immediate success though the cost of the advertising did prove to be more expensive than had been budgeted for. Leadon overcame this problem by the simple expedient of compiling a mailing list of all visitors who actually purchased work (and as many others as was possible) to whom they sent details of forthcoming events. As time passed and the list grew, this supplied a surprisingly good number of responses.

Furthermore, the exhibitions had the added advantage of commencing during the boom years of the mid 1980s. As this boom came to an end there was a marked drop in trade, but fortunately the enterprise had become well enough established to survive.

Today Leadon Fine Arts relies totally on these exhibitions for its trade, such has been its success. There have been no dramatic and ground-breaking strategies in Leadon's marketing history – indeed, it seems they have copied most of their ideas from their competitors. However, there is one thing they have consistently done very right, and that is know their market and know their product.

The company has grown slowly, and could no doubt have done better had more effort been put into a more aggressive marketing strategy. On the other hand this would have involved a far higher capital input and consequently a far higher risk. In all instances Leadon has always followed the low-risk option, which may not appear very exciting to students who have studied the likes of Virgin, Cadburys or any number of other giants. However, it must also be understood that it is this type of approach that is far more common in the commercial world, and with over twenty years behind them who can say it has not worked for Leadon Fine Arts?

ACTIVITIES AND TASKS . . . .

1 Leadon Fine Arts market research would be hard to offload on to a third party. They would need to employ a company that has a very good grasp of the market. Don and his wife obviously needed to consider a number of things before doing it themselves. In the role of Don prepare a checklist of the market. What would he need to consider before attempting to stock higher priced items?

2 The antiques and paintings market is a very specialised one as we have seen. Think about setting up a market stall locally. What would you have to consider before starting up? If you begin your business with no more than £1000 how could you ensure immediate sales and returns on your investment?

3 In the role of an exhibition and event organiser prepare to put on a fair. You should research the following:

a Suitable premises.
b Suitable 'type' of event. Who will be the exhibitors?
c Additional costs – tables, lighting, etc. Are these included in the venue costs?
d Catering.
e Laws relating to public events.
f Charges to be made to each exhibitor.

g Breakeven point.

h Where would you advertise for exhibitors?

i Where would you advertise the event?

j Design simple advertisements for h and i.

k What would be your potential catchment area?

THE THEORY BEHIND IT ALL . . . .

Leadon's change in product to more expensive items brought a potentially dangerous hiccup in their profitability. Pricing is a key component in the success of a business. What exactly is price and how does it relate to product and market? Pricing is placing a value on the product or service. But what actually determines the price?

Price Determinants

- All prices are dependent on the level of demand. If a business can sell a product above what it needs to show a profit, then it will. The basic rules of supply and demand operate in this consideration.

- Competition plays an important part in setting the price. The more suppliers, the lower the price is likely to be. A company must try to double-think the competition and set a price which is both profitable and competitive.

- What is the market segment? Some markets are highly competitive (e.g. foodstuffs), others are not so price sensitive.

- On the subject of price sensitivity, it is often the customer that sets the value attached to a product. This is particularly true in markets like those in which Leadon operates.

- The number of hands that the goods have passed through can determine the end price. Each time a product changes hands a profit is sought and passed on to the next company in the chain.

- Design and development costs are passed on to the consumer. This is particularly true of new and innovative products.

- The costs to produce a product are a key element in its price. The higher the production cost the higher the cost of the product.

- General economic trends such as inflation, interest rates and considerations relating to the workforce (wage levels and productivity) have a direct impact on the price of the product.

Pricing policy

Most companies offer a range of products the prices of which are interrelated. What is their policy regarding price?

- Some products are competitively priced, particularly if they are high volume sellers. The company will accept lower profits per unit as long as the turnover generated is high.
- The concept of a 'loss leader' is often a popular one. One product is offered at just over cost in the hope that it will attract regular custom and entice customers to buy higher profit margin products.
- Cheap and basic products at the bottom end of a market can mean that the company can compete well particularly if the popular image of the product is not very good.
- Price setting is often made by comparing all other products in a product line with one 'key' product. This is invariably the most popular one in the range.
- The after-sales service offered may often offset a highly priced product. Customers are secure in the knowledge that they have good support from the company after the purchase.
- What stage has the product reached in its lifecycle? As a product matures it finds its own price level and levels of demand.

Harbour Designs

Harbour Designs is essentially a one-man operation founded in March 1987 by Gary Sankey. Gary is a fully trained graphic designer who had previously been employed 'in-house' by several large companies where he produced advertising and marketing material. Simply put, his skills (like those of all other graphic designers) lay in producing an 'image' for a client, be that the creation of a company logo or the entire design of a new range of packaging.

His route to self-employment, like many others before him, came as a result of redundancy. The desire had already been there, now the reason (no work) and the wherewithal (redundancy pay) became available.

Gary was doubly fortunate in that his previous employer continued to provide a large amount of freelance work. (This is often the case when people are made redundant and one of the most common ways in which they found their own small businesses.)

Against this background he set out to establish Harbour Designs as a workable independent company. We have decided to concentrate this case study on the period when Gary first started to make a concerted effort to bring in new clients, the period of 1988–89. Previous to this he had obtained clients by word-of-mouth recommendations and had been in truth 'self-employed' rather than a true small businessman.

THE IMAGE . . . .

As a result of his trade, the first thing Gary realised that he had to do was to create a saleable image for his company. (The name Harbour Designs, incidentally, comes from his main hobby of wind surfing.) Unlike many companies with limited funds it was no problem for him to produce a slick presentation since he carried out

HARBOUR
DESIGNS

Palm Tree Buildings, Springhead Enterprise Park,
Northfleet, Kent, DA11 8HB.
Tel:0474-328806, Fax:0474-320285.

GRAPHIC DESIGN
ADVERTISING

most of the work himself. The fruits of his labour can be seen in
Figs 12 and 13.

This package consisted of the normal items of letterhead, business
card, compliments slip and envelope. As well as these set-piece items
he also decided on a number of procedures that he would follow
whenever presenting work to a client. These were to grow into what
is called 'house style' in design jargon. This means, in the case of
Harbour Designs, always presenting work in a particular style of
folder (the actual style is not so important, rather it is the fact that

HARBOUR DESIGNS

Palm Tree Buildings, Springhead Enterprise Park, Northfleet, Kent, DA11 8HB. Tel.0474-328806, Fax.0474-320285.

Gary Sankey
Graphic Designer

Fig 13
The company's artwork folder also promotes the corporate image.

the style remains the same), thereby helping to create an image of continuity and eventually a 'corporate identity'. In this instance it entailed a plain blue package with the simple expedient of attaching a compliments slip to the cover (Fig 13).

The next task was to create a portfolio of work with which to approach prospective clients. The term portfolio refers to a collection of the designer's work that can act as a show case for his or her talents. The construction of such an item is critical to a company's success, particularly when it has no real track record. Gary spent a lot of time and effort getting this package right.

Purely on a presentational level the company opted for the traditional approach of the large leather attaché case with plastic folders inside. The actual contents were another matter and these changed a great deal in the early days as Gary experimented with different combinations.

To start off with, a different list of contents would be put together for each different client, consisting of things that Gary thought they would like. A sensible enough approach, if a little time-consuming, but one that in practice failed – one hesitates to say failed dismally but it was close?

Gary is still not entirely sure why this was so but has put it down to two factors: First, a failure to second-guess correctly the client's likes and dislikes, and secondly a desire on the part of the client to see a variety of work rather than lots of variations on a theme. Later Gary realised that when a client approaches a designer it is often with a view to a long-term relationship, not just for that particular job.

As a result of these experiences the company was faced with two alternatives. It could increase the effort spent on identifying the clients' likes and dislikes, or the nature of the portfolio could be changed. In the light of the second point mentioned above, it was fortuitous for Harbour Designs that it decided to alter the style of the portfolio, though it has to be admitted that this decision was attributable to 50 per cent hunch and 50 per cent lack of resources to carry out the required market research, rather than detailed knowledge of the marketing techniques required.

Armed with these experiences, the portfolio rapidly expanded to be a true showcase of the company's abilities and contained examples (obviously the best in Gary's opinion) of all the different fields it could cope with, i.e. letterheads, advertisements, copywriting, package design and so on. This well-rounded approach provided the company with a far more useful marketing tool than the previous attempt and one that did not require constant updating with each different client.

MAKING CLIENT CONTACTS . . . .

Now, although the portfolio may be a critical part of the marketing process, it can really only be utilised when a face-to-face meeting has been arranged. (It is completely impractical, for example, to use the portfolio itself as a part of a mailshot.) It is therefore necessary to make some kind of customer contact first.

There are a number of options open to the small business-person here, the first and most obvious being the one utilised first by Harbour Designs itself – using contacts already made in previous employment. As already mentioned, these can slowly spread via word of mouth and recommendations. They cannot, however, provide a basis for marketing strategy in their own right. To supplement them the two most common options are the mailshot and telesales, following on to face-to-face meetings and hopefully the conclusion of a deal.

In this respect it quickly became clear that Harbour Designs were somewhat lacking. Being a one-man operation – when additional labour is required it is always obtained via subcontractors – this is perhaps understandable since Gary Sankey would make no claim to being any kind of salesman.

It was revealed that up until six months or so before our interview no concerted and planned effort had been made to establish new customers. Instead there had been a number of piecemeal efforts revolving around a number of mailshots, the addresses for which were taken from local trade directories, the commercial equivalents to the Yellow Pages, and a limited amount of telesales to companies that had been recommended to him in some way.

The mailshots did yield a certain amount of success but were flawed in a number of areas, the most important being in the area of research. Gary had simply looked through the directories and picked out what looked to be middle-sized companies, working on the principle that small companies would not have the funds to employ him and larger ones would be likely already to have the services of a designer. He used the size of the advert employed and that famous 'hunch' when deciding which companies were the right size to approach. Obviously, this system is wildly inaccurate, but, as Gary points out, it was certainly better than nothing. The other major point was his method of addressing the mailshots. In this case he addressed them simply to the 'Managing Director'. It is a generally accepted maxim that if a letter is actually addressed to a specific person there is a far greater chance of someone actually reading it, and it would certainly have paid Harbour Designs to have taken a day to telephone its intended targets and ask to whom it should write the letter. In many cases the telephonist is used to being asked this question and will readily supply the name or department that is relevant.

In January 1991, he at last attempted the first properly planned mailshot campaign following just such a plan. (This is in fact no coincidence since Gary is acquainted with one of the authors!) The results were not stunningly successful, but were certainly superior to his earlier attempts. This also gave Gary the beginnings of a database on potential customers, since in most cases he made follow-up phone calls a few weeks after the mailshot had been sent.

The next stage in the process has already been covered during our discussion on the portfolio. Although the first meeting itself requires a considerable amount of sales skill, in the final analysis it means showing the client the portfolio and hoping that it and the sales pitch persuade them to let Harbour Designs tender for a job.

From here the actual process can vary a great deal, since some clients will decide there and then that this is the company for them and issue a brief. Others decide to give the brief to a number of companies and see which results they like best. We shall assume that this is the case here since it is by far the more common of the two.

THE BRIEF . . . .

A brief received from a client (or potential client) can again vary a great deal but will usually consist of a meeting where the needs and preferences of the company are set out along with what they can afford to pay. Take as an example a magazine advert for a new type of wood veneer to appeal to the DIY enthusiast. The client has enough money to use three colour artwork and has a budget for photography if necessary.

Having received this information, Harbour Designs would then set about putting some ideas down on paper. These preliminary ideas are called 'roughs', for obvious reasons! There can be a number of stages to the roughs depending on the amount of liaison the client requires, but the time will eventually come when the ideas will need to be presented at a meeting (remember here the importance of the 'house style' mentioned earlier). We have now reached the stage at which we are into the realms of sales technique rather than marketing, which is sadly outside the scope of this book.

It is difficult to draw any conclusions on Harbour Designs as yet since it is still too young a company. However, one or two points do stand out. First, we have a classic example of the craftsman going it alone. Gary is a first-rate designer, but at the time he started the company he was in no way a businessman, which is a very common feature of new start-ups. Fortunately for him he had a small but lucrative number of contacts that he had built up before he started the company and which kept him going, but there is no getting away from the fact that his attempts at expanding his customer base were poor.

In many enterprises this would have led to the collapse of the company, but luckily for Gary the quality of his work did to a certain extent make up for this shortcoming. His second saving grace was his own recognition of this problem. Many small businesses literally sit and wait for orders until the receiver arrives, and although he left it late Gary did finally get his act together on this point and is beginning to reap the rewards.

As this chapter is being written he is in the final stages of obtaining an Apple Mackintosh computer to aid him (this piece of equipment alone is worth over £16 000) and he has a turnover fast approaching £100 000 per year.

It is perhaps tempting to ask how well he would be doing if he had had a more commercially aware partner with him at the company's start-up but in the final analysis he has passed the test of all small start-ups in that his company is still here, and relatively thriving, over three years after its conception.

Gary's closing statement to the interview provides perhaps the best way to end this section: 'Erm . . . have you got a designer for the cover of this book yet?'

ACTIVITIES AND TASKS . . . .

1 This activity revolves around putting together a portfolio for a prospective client. For those of you without an artistic bent (and that goes for most of us!), you may use a selection of advertisements which you can find in any magazine or newspaper.

In the role of designer, you have been asked to tender for a job of creating a basic advertisement for a company in the office stationery market. Here are some details of the company:

a The name of the company is D & W Stationery Supplies Ltd.

b It is a family firm which offers basic stationery equipment from paper to office furniture. Essentially, the company operates as a middleman for nearly all the manufacturers of office-related equipment. The customer simply orders the product via the D & W catalogue and supply is guaranteed within 10 days for larger items and 48 hours for small (stock) items.

c The company has a small sales rep team operating in the area that you are in, supported by a telesales team at the industrial unit that serves as the central warehousing and office suite.

d They are installing a freephone facility to encourage more callers. This should be central to your advertisement for them.

e They are looking for ideas for a new advertisement to appear in local newspapers and as flyers to be distributed to local businesses.

f Your portfolio should include similar advertising that will give them ideas as to their new style advertisement.

2 In the role of the marketing/sales manager of D & W Stationery Supplies Ltd, put together a brief for an advertising agency/ designer which reflects what you see as the essentials of your business and how you would like to see it portrayed to potential/existing customers. This brief should be no longer than one side of A4, and it must be clear and straightforward with *no* ambiguous statements.

THE THEORY BEHIND IT ALL . . . .

Choosing someone to do your advertising/design work

This case study brings up the question of choosing the right person for the job, whether it be a designer or an agency. Each have their own advantages and disadvantages. Let's look at the basic questions to ask yourself before offering a job:

● **How important are you to the agency or designer?** If you have a limited budget, then it is perhaps a better idea to pick a smaller company. This will mean more personal attention.

● **Accessibility is vital.** The agency does not have to be on the doorstep necessarily, but travel expenses must be factored in to the cost either at your end or theirs.

● **The 'right fit' approach.** Choose someone who is used to the sort of thing that you want to advertise. Go for an agency that has a track record in the market you are aiming at.

What do you want?

After having decided whether you actually need an agency to do the work for you, it is wise to consider the breadth and experience of the agency. Be precise about what you need:

- Do you need creative help?
- Do you need help in choosing and buying media space?
- Do you need someone to do all the arranging donkeywork?
- Do you need market research?
- Do you need the market analysing?
- Do you need help in targeting your potential customers?

One of the major causes of problems between a client and an agency or designer is the mismatching of needs and skills. Agencies will nearly always say 'yes' to a job. You need to be sure that they can fulfil their end of the work. The Incorporated Society of British Advertisers offer useful guidelines in their booklet *Choosing An Agency*.

Can they do it for you?

The ISBA suggest you look at the following in choosing an agency:

- Just how good is the agency?
- What is its marketing ability?
- What is its knowledge of the market?
- What is its knowledge of the media?
- What specialist skills are there on offer?
- How creative is it?
- Does it offer a full range of skills if needed?
- What is its market research capability?

Making the final choice

Rather like any sort of 'weeding out' process, you will always start with far more choice than is useful. These are some of the approved guidelines in getting down to the final choice of agency:

- Make a short-list of potential agencies.

- You can find these names from many sources, but look to the ISBA and the IPA initially.
- Rule out those that handle competitors – they may well rule *you* out for ethical reasons.
- Get them to perform for you. Get them to give you a presentation of them and their ideas.
- What are they like? Could you work with them now that you have met them?
- How does your organisation get on with them? Are there any sources of friction?

Having gone through this process, you are now in a position to offer the job to one of them. Also, as a useful by-product, you have probably picked up some good 'free' ideas from the losers!

Ark

Ark was established in 1988 by Reg Boorer and Bryn Jones, both of whom were ex-Greenpeace officials who had left that organisation in 1986. Their aim is to produce and market a range of environmentally-friendly household consumables (washing-up liquid, cleaners, etc).

We interviewed Reg, who also works as a freelance consultant and designer for organisations such as the Ramblers Association and for Lynx (see Case study 12) – he is credited with the creation of the 'Roar of Disapproval' slogan for them.

Anita Roddick of Body Shop fame paid for the original research work which culminated in the Ark Manifesto. Early financial backers were also Chrissie Hynes (of the rock group The Pretenders), and Kevin Godley (of 10cc) and his wife.

Ark managed to raise some cash from a bank loan, which paid for the initial Ark environmental video. Further finance was raised (some £60–70 000) by mailshotting a list of celebrities and asking for a £1000 donation to help fund the project. Amongst those who responded were David Bowie, David Puttnam, Sting, Peter Gabriel, Dave Stewart and Dawn French.

So what is Ark? There's no doubt that they are well-connected. When Ark was launched in 1988, they asked its members to follow the 'Ark Pledge' by making small positive changes in their lives which would help safeguard the natural world.

As we will see, they have a very pragmatic approach to affecting the consciousness of the public. They leave it to other organisations to expound a more idealistic and intangible set of concepts about the environment. The key points of the Ark Pledge are:

1 To fit at least two low-energy light bulbs in my home.
2 Not to use my car for short journeys when I could walk.

3 To phone the council and find out where my nearest paper/can/bottle banks are — and use them!

4 To buy products that are kind to our water system — as well as our hands!

5 To buy at least one item of organic food when I shop.

6 To respect Mother Nature.

These individual pledges are easy to comply with. Further than that, Ark even lays out (very kindly) their whole marketing strategy and tells us how to help them achieve their goals:

1 Abide by the pledge — pass copies on to friends.

2 Choose Ark products when you shop.

3 Buy their merchandise (John McEnroe wears their T-shirts).

4 Buy their campaign packs and start campaigning yourself.

5 Recruit just five members for Ark.

6 Be green at work or school.

7 Organise fund-raising events for Ark.

8 Become a friend.

9 Get your company to support Ark. (They operate a corporate pledge and membership division.)

10 Make a donation.

In line with the background of the founders, the ten levels of involvement are easy and straightforward. Taking a leaf out of the business world's book, they make cut-out response forms easy to fill in, and the language is simple and uncomplicated.

ARK PRODUCTS . . . .

One of the points in the pledge was to use household products with minimum impact on the environment. There was only one drawback — these products were not readily available in supermarkets at affordable prices. This led to Ark's decision to market its own range of products.

Since then, 'green consumerism' has become an undeniable market force, and many manufacturers have followed suit by introducing — or adapting — products to meet consumers' growing environmental concerns. Nonetheless, Ark continues to set higher standards by refining existing products and introducing new ones.

Ark products are also used as campaigning tools. Wherever possible,

YOU CAN HELP

THERE'S NOTHING mysterious about issues such as global warming, pollution or ozone depletion. They are simply **symptoms** of a planet that is sickening.

And like any good doctor, if we want to restore the earth to full health we must begin by tackling the **causes** of that sickness.

That's where we, as individuals, come in. Because many of the major environmental problems we face are caused by the lifestyles we lead.

Each of us can make some simple, sensible changes in our lives to lessen our personal impact on the natural environment.

And Ark can help. Ark's sole aim is to help people lead 'greener' lives. It's not a pressure group. It doesn't lobby government or industry. And it doesn't claim to be able to save the world for you!

Quite simply, Ark is a Registered Charity that provides you with the information and practical means you need to start caring for the environment *yourself*.

That's why you'll see Ark environmentally-responsible products on the shelves in major stores. Ark *is not* a commercial company-but it recognises that people need practical, affordable alternatives if we are to cut down on pollution in a real way.

What's more, every time you buy one of the products, a few pence goes to Ark.

Like all charities, Ark desperately needs funds to continue its work. You can help Ark-and the environment -by choosing Ark products when you shop. You can help fund Ark's work by buying some of the literature and merchandise overleaf.

Above all, you can help by following the Ark Pledge-and taking the first step on the road to a healthier, more beautiful earth.

Our children may never see the earth as we have known it. The oceans, soil and atmosphere are poisoned. Our own health too, is failing.

Yet even so, the vast majority of people in this country remain uninvolved in the fight for life on earth, untouched by the real urgency of the environmental crisis.

We are at a turning point in the history of life on earth. If we wish to guarantee the health and survival of future generations - if we wish to change the world for the better - then we must start by changing ourselves.

Pledge yourself today to strive for a healthier, more beautiful world. This is Ark's purpose. There is no greater cause, nor one that so demands the support of every thinking, caring man and woman.

Ark

The printing of this leaflet has been very kindly sponsored by CMB Ltd.

Fig 14 Exploiting the green market – a page of one of Ark's product leaflets.

they carry information about the environmental issues relating to that product – and all the profits that Ark makes from sales are covenanted to the registered charity, the Ark Environmental Foundation.

Above all, Ark products are designed to break through the so-called 'inertia barrier'. For millions of people, choosing an Ark product over a conventional brand may be the first 'green action' they have ever taken.

Ark takes the point of view that 'we are all part of the problem'. It recognises that individual action from consumers has to be the first step in addressing the environmental crisis we have on our hands, created by our own hands. In other words they adopt the 'bottom-up' approach – their plan is to get to the 90 per cent of the public not fully aware of the eco-problem.

Paradoxically it was Margaret Thatcher's 'Green speech' of the 1980s that set the ball rolling as far as supermarkets taking the issue seriously was concerned. Ark understood that success depended largely on the following:

1 Consistency in philosophy behind all decisions.
2 Affordability of products.

Fig 15
Paula Yates and Bob Geldof – the choice of endorsee can radically affect the product's marketing.

3 The products needed to be 'recognisably normal'.
4 High-profile celebrity endorsement.

For the last point, they enlisted the support of three well-known couples, pictured holding the products: Linda and Paul McCartney, Dawn French and Lenny Henry, and Paula Yates and Bob Geldof.

In line with their policy they would like to reduce the range of products in the Ark line. Most products could be multi-purpose, but consumers have not yet responded to this notion. It is a constant battle to keep their place in the supermarkets. For every product that has space on the shelves, there are dozens more vying for that space. It is this pressure, in the main, that makes Ark's next move crucial.

A product range that was launched recently was a disappointing failure for them. The Ark paint range aimed at the DIY superstores failed to make a significant impact on the market. Throughout the recession this particular market has been hit very hard, and this factor alone seems to be the major reason behind the poor showing.

However, Ark looks to the future with confidence and industry, and hopes to forge links with companies on a consultancy basis to help them move towards environmentally friendly products and a more thoughtful approach to their production methods.

Reg sums up Ark's philosophy, which amply shows the difference between Ark and many of the other environmental groups, as follows:

'My dream is that the Ark brand-name is as well-known as Coke by the end of the century . . . The Green movement has nailed its colours to the mast . . . we take a more pragmatic approach.'

ARK MERCHANDISING . . . .

Like most charitable organisations Ark offers a full range of merchandising products whose sales are vital to their continued success. Their campaign kits on household waste (suggesting ways of cutting down on what you put in the bin) and their Streetwise (car emissions and fuel saving – which involves a tie-in with Hertz) are self-contained and accessible, consisting of badges, stickers, posters and so on. Other key merchandising include T-shirts, badges, booklets, videos and guides.

Image plays a big role here. The Ark logo is very visible on all products and features the latest trends in design techniques.

THE ART OF TRAVELLING LIGHT . . . .

The Art of Travelling Light campaign has a threefold purpose and marks a move away from UK-based activity by Ark to exporting ideas about the environment via the tourist industry. It aims to re-educate us about the countries we travel to, to help those inhabitants of the country to accept us and to make us aware of what we are doing to the environment through visiting foreign countries. This 'responsible tourist' campaign is funded jointly by the EC, Manchester Airport and Thompson Travel. It is fronted by the celebrity Sue Pollard, who appears in the video advertising feature.

The campaign is light-hearted and upbeat, and reaches the public in two main ways: Thompson's inflight magazine (a 16-page colour magazine) features the campaign, and the video will be shown to the 6½ million passengers carried by Britannia Airways over the year. The advertisement is also featured in the magazine press, and an illustrated advert carrying a still from the video appeared in *Sky Magazine*'s Christmas 1991 issue.

art of the
dvertisement for the
rt of Travelling Light.

The last thing you want when you go on holiday is to be weighed down with everything but the kitchen sink. Where's the fun in that?

If you're going abroad on holiday this year, read 'GOING FOR IT'. Find out how you can lighten the load on yourself, on your hosts, and on the environment. Join Ark for just £1 and we'll send you a copy free.

☐ YES, I want to join Ark and help protect the planet. I enclose a cheque/PO for £1.

☐ I enclose a donation of £_____

NAME

ADDRESS

_____

_____

POSTCODE

Ark PO Box 1784 London W9 3QW

But sometimes the heaviest burden of all is in our heads.

In our attitudes. In our preconceived ideas.

In the cultural junk we carry with us.

This summer, leave your excess baggage behind. Discover the art of travelling light.

The Ark Environmental Foundation
is a registered charity No. 1000257

It is indeed amazing that, despite the recession, the Gulf War and other prominent news items, Ark managed to get enough sponsorship finance together to launch the campaign.

The second phase of the campaign (at the time of writing still awaiting a sponsor) is the Children's Green Passport Pack, which includes activities and games and a small phrase book. This is aimed at the young market, and is given free (or for a small donation) so that children too can get involved in learning about the culture of the country they are in and increase their awareness of the environment.

ARK AND THE FUTURE

Ark is planning hard for the next century. They intend to develop their range of products as mentioned earlier, but also have other major commitments:

1 **To move into the American market** This may prove difficult as there are a number of existing organisations working there. Links with them may be a more viable alternative.
2 **To establish a chain of franchised Ark vegetarian fast-food outlets** This poses a huge potential planning and execution problem, but will offer enormous high-street exposure.
3 **To seek new sponsorship deals** This is with a view to increased exposure in the mass media.
4 **To develop the concept of the Ark Seal of Approval for products and processes** The hope is that Ark will be a type of standard against which products will be judged for their environmental impact.

ACTIVITIES AND TASKS

1 In the role of Reg Boorer write a press release for a range of Ark Photodegradable Bin Liners. This should be suitable for inclusion in women's magazines and another publication that caters for regular shoppers.

2 Ark is attempting to convince companies to consider the environment when producing products. In the role of a public relations director of a large car manufacturer, prepare a response refuting any allegations that your company is not environmentally aware. To help you do this, contact two or three manufacturers and ask them what they are doing in this area.

3 In the role of Reg Boorer devise a new campaign and short-list a selection of companies that could sponsor the campaign. You should consider the following in your choice of companies:

a Relevance of campaign to company.
b Relative size of company to competitors.
c Companies involved should not be competitors in any way (think laterally – supplier, wholesaler, retailer).
d Exactly what the company can get out of the sponsorship.

THE THEORY BEHIND IT ALL . . . .

Two main issues arise out of this case study on Ark. The first is the green marketing question, or more broadly, social marketing. The second is that of the nature of non-profit-making organisations and how they function in the business environment.

Social marketing

Social marketing itself has defied attempts to give it a meaningful definition. The boundaries of it are forever moving. Let's be brave! Social marketing implies that a company should act in conjunction with the public interest by attempting to serve the needs and demands of society, at the same time as making a profit. It goes further though – consumers place a value on their quality of life as well as the quality of the product that they are purchasing. This is well illustrated by two examples:

1 **Cosmetics** If you have looked ahead to the Cosmetics To Go case study (see Case study 11), you will already be aware of the issues, but essentially consumers are now horrified to learn of the suffering of animals for our vanity.
2 **Cigarette smoking** Lower tar brands have increased in sales whilst other brands have suffered. Despite this the growing trend towards smoke-free zones and smoke-free offices continues apace.

The wider issues are those that concern the likes of Ark:

● Pollution
● Congestion in cities
● Waste levels and disposal
● Deforestation
● Dangerous working conditions

Boundaries and responsibilities

If the principle task of marketing is to satisfy the needs of the consumer in an efficient and profitable way, can this be done with regard to social responsibility? Some questions arise:

- Is it enough to produce safe products?
- Is honesty in advertising sufficient?
- Is commitment to pollution reduction enough?
- Why should we take the lead and the costs?

Many now think that marketing has a new responsibility. Since it can and does affect consumers' attitudes, why not change their attitudes towards social responsibility? Can marketing afford to be involved when profit is the key goal?

It is certainly true that a company which incorporates a social angle to its activities will reap a rich harvest. Companies are beginning to respond and are mobilising their efforts to develop social roles. Indeed, the government may soon make them if they do not move fast enough. Adopting a considerate attitude to the environment may well not be an option but a requirement. Some safety measures may well increase prices and companies must be wary of the effects that this will have on their business. They will be quick to blame government legislation if this is the case.

Non-profit-making or non-loss organisations

We have deliberately adopted this two-fold definition, since the organisations which fall into this category can be very efficient in profit-making. The key difference is what they do with the profits. How exactly do they differ from normal business concerns?

- **They may have a less clear set of objectives** After all, a commercial business is concerned with profit and profit alone.
- **Attracting resources can be a big problem** The public are often reluctant to give money for something that does not give them a tangible return (hence the popularity of merchandising products from charities).
- **Balancing of priorities** What is important and what is crucial? A hard decision for a charity.
- **How do you measure success?**
- **Dealing with political pressures** Political standpoints (especially if contrary to the current government) can adversely affect income/grants, exposure and endorsements.

Sunsetters

Sunsetters is a direct result of the development of a business begun in 1989 by Chris Dunnet and Caleb Pringle. The partnership is principally a typesetting operation whose business is acquired by two main routes:

1 Someone comes into the shop with a design idea for a leaflet, brochure, catalogue, etc., which they would like printed. Chris and Caleb then put the words and designs together into a form that can be printed.
2 Someone asks them to word-process a large amount of text into a form that can be printed as a book.

During his last year at university, Chris had to write a dissertation. Not being the most dedicated of students, he decided that if the presentation of the project was good it might hide the content! It worked. So why not offer the service to others? With this germ of an idea, the typesetting business began.

Computer-aided typesetting and design was becoming an acceptable medium at the time that Sunsetters were setting up their business. With some investment from a 'sleeping' partner, they started work from a room in Chris's flat. The problem was that typesetting had been something of a closed shop, but the computer boom meant that 'amateurs' could also offer a viable alternative that meant the customer did not have to pay a designer, say, £60 per hour. Like many other small operations, Sunsetters could undercut this price.

Within the last three years Sunsetters did expand into print work, but the recession hit the print business very hard so they eventually sold their stake in the printing firm and returned to being a two-man operation. They have now also established a 'bespoke' computer business, making custom-made packages of hard- and software for particular clients.

Sunsetters consider themselves to be a service industry, and have identified three main client groups:

1 **Book publishers** Those who need text formatted into book form. This is highly structured and requires little creativity. The end job price is relatively high, however.

2 **Middlemen in the print business** This is mainly design work, typesetting and layout ideas. This can be very lucrative. Sunsetters lay out and design a variety of brochures, sales leaflets and fliers which have been passed on to them by a printer. The printer pays Sunsetters for the work they do, and charges that cost (with a mark-up) on to the end-user customer.

3 **Off-street customers** People come in and ask for a job to be done, e.g. CVs and business cards. These jobs are numerous and cheap, but pay the rent!

Targeting each of the three different types of customer requires a different approach. In particular they have worked hard in servicing their book publishing clients. Sunsetters' main book client is Bowker-Saur, a subsidiary of Reed International. It has taken Sunsetters the full three years of their existence to achieve a position in which they are considered 'reliable' enough to handle all of Bowker-Saur's typesetting. They began their sales campaign with a very useful personal contact. The publisher first tested out Sunsetters' ability with small jobs, building finally to the point where they know that all typesetting will go through them. Sunsetters (at the time of our interview) had no less than five 350-page books to set for Bowker-Saur! They also handle their promotional material for leaflets. Chris recognises that this gradual build-up involved a lot of hard work and a number of 'loss leaders' (jobs at reduced prices or work not charged at full price), in order to gain their confidence and reliance.

SETTING UP, RUNNING AND MARKETING A 'PRINT SHOP'

Sunsetters began as an 'amateur' set-up in Chris's flat. They then had the fortune to be offered space at the front of a client's shop in Lexington Street in the West End of London. The client needed a small regular rental income as well as the opportunity to use a typesetter 'in house' for work passing through his business. The owner of the premises was what is called a 'print-farmer' – in other words, a printing middleman. Work comes in from his range of customers and the middleman places the print work with one of a variety of printers that are subcontracted. The print-farmer adds his or her costs and profit margins to the price quoted by the printer, and the end-user pays the print-farmer, who then pays the printer. This is a common way of getting print work done.

LETTERHEADS AND IMAGE . . . .

The idea for the name came out of the desire to sound different, perhaps fun. The first idea, 'Redsetters', was thrown out – people might have thought it was a dog kennel! Sunsetters' logo is simple and appealing, uncluttered, but clever.

Fig 16
Sunsetters' logo, used
on their letterhead.

ESTABLISHING A CLIENT BASE . . . .

The offer of premises in Lexington Street was an excellent opportunity – not only was there a guarantee of a certain amount of work, but there was also the advantage of a high profile in the front of a retail shop, right in the heart of a publishing and business area. The chances of getting plenty of passing trade were enormous.

Getting a large enough client base, however, can take time. So how do you manage to show potential customers what desk-top publishing is capable of? Well, you do your own letterheads, your own business cards and your own advertising material. You then use this as a basis for your own portfolio of material to show potential customers. If your manner is right – and, of course, your price – they will give you a chance.

Taking care with deadlines and the quality of the work, you can then try for bigger and more lucrative jobs with the client. Credibility is hard won, and very easy to lose. The key to success is to make sure that it is not you that is holding up the process. As Sunsetters take more and more responsibility for finishing a job, they have more control over the deadlines. But if they then take on a job and make mistakes, that inevitably means no more work from that customer.

Deadlines on work can vary from six months to a matter of an hour. With long-term work it is the usual procedure to stagger the invoicing as stages of the work are finished. This arrangement is crucial for a reasonable cash-flow.

MARKETING AND ADVERTISING . . . .

This is variable, but falls roughly into the following categories:

1 **Word of mouth** Working as they do in a very active area business-wise, even a drink in the local pub can bring business in. All clients are treated as valuable commodities, as they in turn can recommend Sunsetters to others in whatever business they work in. Sunsetters never underestimate the value of word of mouth.

2 **Passing trade** This is variable, depending upon the number of people passing the shop and what percentage of them are in a position to place printing and typesetting work. In any event, Chris and Caleb always put the most attractive looking job on the computer nearest the window so that passers-by can at least see what they are doing. In some cases this works, and does bring in prospective clients.

3 **Specific targeting** They recognised that existing print shops in the West End did not actually produce anything themselves (except photocopying perhaps). They would take in jobs and subcontract all the work elsewhere. Sunsetters visited each of the print shops and offered them a quick-turn-around typesetting service.

4 **Businesses which had computer systems** The average secretary, whilst able to word-process, could not use the desk-top publishing packages. Sunsetters advertised in *Ms London*, a free paper given away at all the central London tube and rail stations, offering their services as trainers. The advertisement cost just £40. Amazingly, they got nearly eighty calls over the space of two years! They never repeated the advertisement, they simply didn't need to. In the first six months Sunsetters grossed nearly £3000 from the one advertisement. This client base also helped in other sales, such as printing work, computer software and consultancy work.

5 **Geographical targeting** Thousands of people use the tube stations

around the area that Sunsetters operate in. Both Chris and Caleb stand outside a tube station at least two mornings a week (from about 8.30 a.m. to 9.30 a.m.) and hand out leaflets.

6 **Trade journals** This has proved very unsuccessful. *Offset Reproduction & Litho*, a printers' magazine, was tried, but most printers have their own typesetting operations. Desk-top publishing was seen as more of a threat than a service that they would like to use. Three or four hundred pounds per advertisement is very hard to justify, both in terms of levels of response and expected immediate turnover.

7 **Specific people within an organisation** Personal contact with those who make printing decisions such as marketing, production and design are the key areas. The initial contact is usually made by telephone to the secretary of the potential target, a letter is then sent followed up by a call a couple of days later direct to the target with the aim of arranging a meeting.

About 50 per cent of the business is repeat custom, which has its own set of problems. It is easy for a small business to go under taking on repeat business from their clients if they do not take account of the amount of credit that they give them. This has been for Sunsetters, and no doubt many other businesses, a recurring problem.

There is always enough 'down-time' on a long-term project to allow work on quick-turnover projects. This means that, hopefully, there are always 'cash sales' coming in whilst the longer-term invoiced work is underway.

PERSONAL SELLING AND CLOSING A SALE . . . .

Sunsetters arranged an initial meeting with the Production Controller of Bowker-Saur, principally to explain the range of services available and Sunsetters' own capabilities. Unless they could prove their skills they could not hope to get any work, since the publishers already were dealing with several typesetters. They were given a series of tasks, several sample chapters were given to Sunsetters to typeset, and, of course, a deadline.

Not only this, they had to create a competitive pricing structure in order to be attractive to the publisher. Fortunately, as Chris says, 'that was all there was to it' – rather an understatement, since the problems of dealing with a large piece of work from a new potential client are difficult, to say the least. However, the exercise worked out well for Sunsetters and the publishers. Within a week or so the former had a year's contract for typesetting, and the latter had a good reliable service at a competitive rate.

Sunsetters' location worked in their favour – being only fifteen

Fig 17
One of Sunsetters'
publications.

minutes from the publisher obviously helped. Chris also asserts that their attitude of 'Yes, we can do that,' as well as their willingness to take over the more onerous tasks of production played a part.

NEW BUSINESS, NEW IDEAS · · · · · · · · · · · · · · ·

Two of the latest pieces of work undertaken by Sunsetters show the broad nature of their work and the flexibility needed to be able to turn their hand to almost any job that comes up:

- 'The Dance Theatre of Egypt' was a hand-bill job acquired through one of Sunsetters' printer contacts. This was a simple job, involving the use of their Pagemaker software.
- *The Street* magazine (illustrated in Fig 17) is a bi-monthly 32-page professional 'fanzine' for Coronation Street devotees. It currently takes around twenty hours per week of input from Sunsetters.

Since our interview, Sunsetters has moved to more prestigious offices in Tottenham Court Road. They have secured further publishing contracts, and have diversified into the hardware/software market with a range of their own bespoke computer systems.

ACTIVITIES AND TASKS · · · · · · · · · · · · · · · · ·

1 In the role of Chris and Caleb, attempt to schedule the following work over the space of a week. You should assume the following:

a They have two computer systems.

b A 'normal day' runs from 9a.m. to 6p.m.

c They have ongoing work as detailed below.

d Chris will be out visiting potential clients on the following days:

- Tuesday 10a.m.–2p.m.
- Wednesday 3p.m.–5p.m.
- Thursday 8a.m.–10p.m.

e Chris also needs to visit the printer to pick up work due for collection by a client by Friday morning (11a.m.). This will take him two hours for the round trip.

This is a list of the ongoing work:

a For Bowker-Saur 6 hours of work to be ready by Thursday lunchtime.

b Six pages of *The Street* to be ready by Friday morning (10.30a.m.). Each page will take 45 minutes.

c A twenty-page report for a local firm of solicitors. Each page will take half an hour.

Short-term work:

a Arrives Tuesday 3p.m. – 50 laser copies of a leaflet (2 hours). Needed by Wednesday 4p.m.

b Arrives Wednesday 11p.m. – 1500 photocopies to be copied and collated (3 hours). Needed by Thursday 4p.m.

c Arrives Wednesday 10.30p.m. – design work on a letterhead for an artist, two hundred copies required (2½ hours). Needed by Friday 1p.m.

Passing trade (needed immediately):

a Monday 11a.m. – photocopying 2000 copies (2 hours).

b Monday 3p.m. – CV for a student, twenty copies (1½ hours).

c Tuesday 10.30a.m. – 50 photocopies (½ hour).

d Wednesday 11a.m. – brochure design (needed within 4 hours, takes 2 hours).

e Wednesday 12.30p.m. – 250 photocopies (½ hour).

f Thursday 9a.m. – 500 business cards (1 hour on computer, 2 hours plus 2 hour trip to printers).

g Friday 10a.m. – 2000 photocopies and collation (3 hours), needed by 6p.m.

If there's any time, Chris can spend it phoning up sales leads. He has eleven of these and they will take about 20 minutes each. And by the way, forget lunch hours, there's never any time – there is a sandwich bar next door!

2 In the role of Chris and Caleb devise a hand-bill for distribution outside the stations in the West End. If you have access to a desk-top publishing package try to format one. You should allow yourself no longer than one hour!

THE THEORY BEHIND IT ALL . . . .

Chris and Caleb, as Sunsetters, cater for both the consumer market and the trade market. They can be very different targets to aim at. However, the service which they offer provides the opportunity to blur the distinctions a little. Let's look at the theoretical considerations when communicating with the two markets, bearing in mind that they are not really as clear-cut as you may have once thought.

Consumer markets

Communicating with this market involves the following considerations:

- Telling the customer about the product or service.
- Correcting any misconceptions that they might have about you or the product/service.
- Getting the customer to buy from you more often.
- Reminding the customer that you still exist.
- Offering customers any special deals or promotions you are running.
- Educating the customer about a product or service.
- Building your company image.
- Building a product or service image.
- Building up customer loyalty.

Trade markets

Some communications are very similar to those to the consumer market, but particular to the trade are the following types of message:

- Provision of information about your company in general.
- In-depth information about your products/services.
- Warnings of forthcoming changes in products/services and operational procedures.
- Trade incentives and offers.
- Educating the trade on the use of your products/services.

Targeting

Not all of your communications are going to get to the right person, but setting target objectives is the first step in cutting costs and making your attempts much more effective:

- Who are you aiming the message at?
- What information do they need to help make up their minds?

- How much is it going to cost you?
- How big should your budget be?
- How do you apportion the costs?
- How can you evaluate all of this?

Having identified the target by addressing the points above, you can then consider the following:

- Once you have identified the target, by what methods can you ensure that they are interested in what you have to say?
- How can you maximise your spending? Just how cost-effective is it?
- How much of the information that you wish to communicate can be done in ways which do not cost you anything? Can you secure editorial space? Can you get business by referrals from other companies?

Costs

Above all what you do must be affordable, perhaps related in some way to the sales revenue (sometimes it is a fixed percentage). You must also be flexible, in as much as you must be able to react to the competition quickly. More often than not, however, companies will fix their spending in relation to very clearly defined objectives and targets.

Boxtree

Boxtree are book publishers founded in 1986 by Sarah Mahaffy. The original, major shareholders were TVS (TV South) who sold the business to Reed Exhibitions in 1989. This was to be a relatively short ownership since Sarah had independence in mind.

The buy-out team consisted of Sarah (who used to work for Macmillan), Adrian Sington (ex-Collins and Penguin) and David Inman (also ex-Macmillan), who together put up 30 per cent of the necessary finance. Finance Director, Christine Brown, and Peter Roche, the Non-executive Chairman, both joined them. The remaining capital was supplied by investors Ventureforth.

Fig 18
Book cover for a TV tie-in.

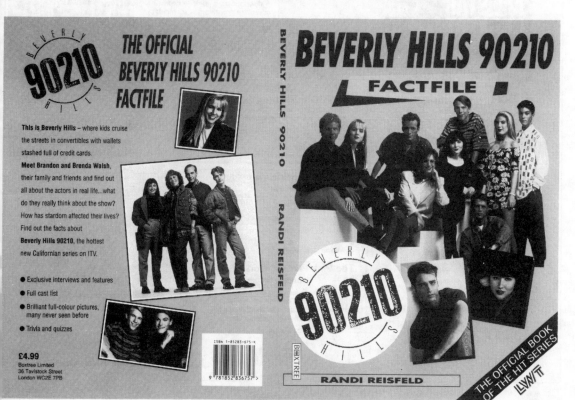

Based in Tavistock Street, Covent Garden, Boxtree publish mainly TV tie-in books, which was Sarah's background and main interest over the past few years. Early Boxtree publications included *Art of*

BOOKS PUBLISHED IN ASSOCIATION WITH TV Times

Supersoaps
Chris Stacey and Darcy Sullivan

A popular illustrated book on the soap operas watched by millions of viewers all around the world — Coronation Street, Crossroads, Dallas, Dynasty, Brookside, Emmerdale Farm, East Enders and Neighbours.

160 pp, 280×200mm, 32 col, 100 b and w photos

1 85283 206 1 £8.95 hb

Chris Stacey and Darcy Sullivan

TV's Greatest Hits
Anthony Davis

What makes a TV programme sell all over the world? What is the secret of the success of Phil Silvers, The Avengers and The Lone Ranger? This book makes fascinating reading as satellite and cable bring 'cult' shows from the sixties to a new generation of viewers.

160 pp, 280×200mm, 32 col, 100 b and w photos

1 85283 237 1 £12.95 hb 10 November

The ITV Encyclopedia of Adventure
Dave Rogers

A discriminating guide to nearly 200 adventure programmes screened on ITV in the last 30 years.

593 pp, 234×156mm, 75 b and w photos

1 85283 217 7 £9.95 pb
1 85283 205 3 £15.95 hb

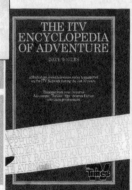

THE ITV ENCYCLOPEDIA OF ADVENTURE

DAVE ROGERS

All Star Cookery
Jill Cox

Eat breakfast with the stars of TV-am, lunch with Bobby Davro, and dine with Michael Barrymore. Over 250 recipes. Based on the cookery feature published weekly in TVTimes. ★ Circulation 3.2 million.

128 pp, 282×250mm, 60 col photos

1 85283 238 X £10.95 hb 6 October

The James Bond Bedside Companion
Raymond Benson
The Complete Guide to the World of 007

The first book to examine all aspects of the James Bond phenomenon — the author, the novels and the films.

272 pp, 280×216mm, 100 b and w photos

1 85283 233 9 £9.95 pb
1 85283 234 7 £14.95 hb 15 September

The Pink Panther Work Out Book
Bridget Woods

An exercise book featuring the much-loved cartoon character, The Pink Panther, with a full programme of exercises by the director of London's world-famous Fitness Centre, Bridget Woods.

BY BRIDGET WOODS

96 pp, 198×198mm, 50 col, 100 b and w illus

1 85283 215 0 £5.95 hardcover
1 85283 218 5 £59.50 (ten copy counterpack)

Fig 19 (opposite)
Trade marketing leaflet
showing new
publications.

the Western World, Inside the Bank of England, Go Fishing with John Wilson, Survival, and Best of Treasure Hunt.

Concentrating on TV tie-ins not only cashes in on the popularity of current programmes, but also provides plenty of free promotion on the TV when the book is mentioned at the end of a programme. Their Christmas 1991 releases include The Killer Tomatoes, The Simpsons and Beverly Hills 90210.

Boxtree secured the rights to produce a great many new titles over the past year in the face of severe competition from much larger and longer established publishers. These include:

- The Golden Girls
- Cheers
- Thirtysomething
- LA Law
- Street Cred (about Coronation Street)
- Poddington Peas
- New Kids on the Block (a series of novels)
- American Tail 2
- Dinosaur!

How did they manage this success? Sarah Mahaffy is cautiously confident about the future:

'We've had a very promising start. Our turnover for the first six months was just over a million and we have a very strong list coming up. Of course we're aware of the recession, but the whole point about Boxtree is that the titles have the benefit of some media coverage. So while we know the recession is there, we don't think it's affecting us too much. We're quietly confident that we'll swim through it.'

HE LAUNCHING OF THE BILL . . . .

We are going to concentrate on the launch of The Bill book by Boxtree and the job of their Publicity Manager, Nichola Motley. Nichola is in her mid-twenties, and an English and Drama honours graduate. She began working for Boxtree as a receptionist/ secretary/publicity assistant. These 'catch-all' introductory jobs are often the stepping stones to bigger and better employment in the publishing world. In a short while she became their Publicity

Manager. Her job responsibilities are wide-ranging and demanding, including:

- Arranging interviews for TV and radio.
- Organising launch parties for books.
- Maintaining Boxtree's list of reviewers.
- Setting up features on their books in magazines and newspapers.
- Selling serialisation rights to newspapers and magazines (this involves allowing them to print parts of a book).
- Author tours of the country.
- Collecting and distributing press cuttings about Boxtree books.
- Contact-making with TV companies and reporters.
- Writing marketing plans for specific books.
- Organising sales conferences.
- Arranging Boxtree's stand at trade fairs.
- Keeping the sales representatives up to date with publicity information about new books and future plans.
- Maintaining Boxtree's database (which contains over 800 useful contacts to help promote books).

Nichola talked us through the launching of Boxtree's *The Bill* book, which amply shows exactly what is involved in the launching of a new product:

1 An initial marketing meeting was called which involved all Boxtree staff concerned with the book – sales, publicity, editorial, etc.
2 Out of the marketing meeting arose a basic marketing plan which looked like the plan detailed opposite.

Some of the items in the plan need a little explanation:

a Number of plugs refers to the number of free mentions of the book after an episode of the series.
b Review copy distribution refers to the maximum (although alterable) number of free copies to be given out to reviewers on the database. The figure quoted usually includes about 50–60 copies given out to reviewers, and some 30–40 given out for competition prizes.
c Serialisation refers to allowing a newspaper to print an extract from the book, in return for a cash fee.
d Second serialisation refers to allowing magazines to print similar extracts to those already offered to a newspaper but which cater for a different market. Again a cash fee is required.
3 The manuscript (just the text and possibly some illustrations in rough form) is sent to the features editors of likely serialisation

MARKETING PLAN

Title: THE BILL

TV details: ITV – Tuesdays and Thursdays
Duration – 30 minutes
Time – 8.00–8.30p.m.
Ratings – 10 million viewers
Number of plugs – 10

Trade advertising: *Publishing News*

Co-operative advertising: W H Smith's Christmas catalogue and Menzies' Christmas catalogue.

Review copy distribution: 100.

PR:

National newspapers – possible serialisation in *The People*, *News of the World*, the *Sun* and the *Daily Mirror*.

Regional newspapers – features and reviews in *Birmingham Evening Mail*, *Middlesborough Evening Gazette*, *Newcastle Journal* and *The Yorkshire Evening Post* (plus others to be arranged).

Magazines – second serialisation in *Woman's Own*, *Woman's Realm* or *Woman*. Features, reviews and giveaways in *Radio Times*, *TV Times*, *What's On TV* and *Me*.

Radio – competitions and reviews on LBC, GLR and key independent and BBC stations including CNFM (Cambridge).

takers. In this instance, the *Daily Mirror* took serialisation rights (which appeared some three weeks prior to the book being published), and *Me* magazine took second serialisation rights (which appeared the month that the book was published).

4 Liaison was arranged with the TV company involved in the production of the programme, in this case with Thames Television's Wendy Tayler. Thames would become involved in organising events which would need the attendance of the cast of the programme and supplying photographs and promotional material.

5 The Piccadilly branch of Dillons expressed an interest in hosting the launch of the book (see small flyer distributed to reporters and the media in general). This would be a joint operation between

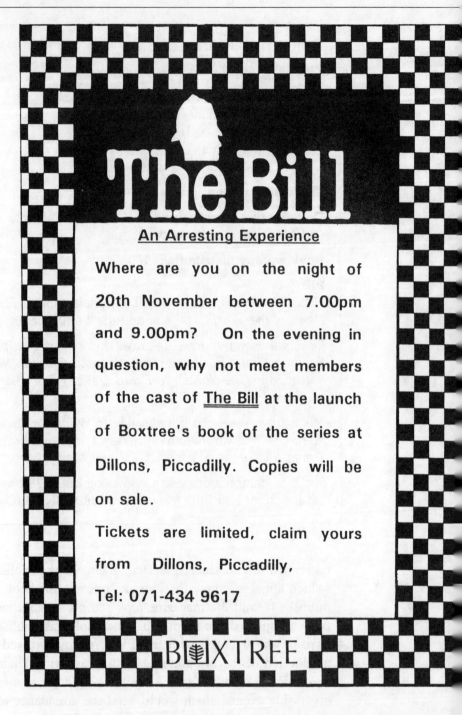

The Bill

An Arresting Experience

Where are you on the night of 20th November between 7.00pm and 9.00pm?   On the evening in question, why not meet members of the cast of The Bill at the launch of Boxtree's book of the series at Dillons, Piccadilly. Copies will be on sale.

Tickets are limited, claim yours from   Dillons, Piccadilly,

Tel: 071-434 9617

BOXTREE

**Fig 20
An example of
publicity for a new
book launch.**

Boxtree, Thames Television and Dillons, although the bulk of the work would devolve to Nichola. The launch was a great success and some twenty of the cast turned up, but unfortunately the evening clashed with the launch of Michael Jackson's new single!

6 Copies of the book arrive at the warehouse some six weeks prior to launch. Immediately, Nichola dispatches the reviewers' list to the warehouse which then send out copies as required to:

a literary editors of magazines and national newspapers;

b literary and features editors of Sunday newspapers;

c magazines – mainly the weeklies since monthly magazines have too long a lead time to get the book into an issue close to the launch date;

d radio – local to London mainly, both independent and BBC. Nichola organised a feature on Gloria Hunniford's radio show and also on Derek Jamieson's;

e specialist magazines and relevant journals, in this instance *The Job* (the magazine for the police);

f TV magazine programmes – TV-AM featured a slot on the book.

7 Free copies and competitions for various magazines are organised, as pre-arranged by Nichola, in:

a *Look In*

b *Fast Forward*

c *Number One*

d *Smash Hits*

e *Just 17*

These younger age group magazines were chosen as the series appeals to the younger market. The competitions involve sending some five or six (preferably signed) copies of the book as prizes for a simple competition.

Nichola also managed to organise competitions in *TV Times* and *Radio Times* which also offered signed copies of the book as prizes.

8 Members of the cast which had a particular link with any part of the country were featured on the relevant local radio station or in personal visits to bookstores in the area.

9 Nichola also managed to get ten free plugs for the book at the end of episodes during the launch period.

That's about it! Nichola was also working on at least another five or six books at the same time as this. We were grateful for her time, squeezed in en route to her evening off at a Karaoke Night!

ACTIVITIES AND TASKS . . . .

1 In the role of Nichola plan how you would launch one of the following:

a a book based on *Coronation Street*;
b a book based on *Star Trek: The Next Generation*;
c a book about making TV programmes.

You should start by writing a basic marketing plan like Nichola had done for *The Bill* and go through the stages before launch. You should begin your timetable some three months before the launch.

2 Nichola has an extensive database of useful names and contacts. In the role of publicity manager for a book publisher prepare a list of useful contacts (some thirty or so) that you could regularly send material to about new books. *BRAD* may be a useful source.

3 Nichola often has to design the competitions for her new books. Design one for one of your favourite TV programmes that would be usable for the list of teen-magazines mentioned in the case study. You should offer no more than five or six copies for each individual competition.

THE THEORY BEHIND IT ALL . . . .

The Boxtree case study brings up a number of useful points. We shall concentrate, however, on how products are launched and media planning.

Launching a product

Launching a product can be very expensive, so the development and market research needs to be accurate. TV costs are enormous, and promotional costs, including posters, sales promotions and incentives to stockists, can cost as much as half the total revenue that the product can generate in the first year. Manufacturers are looking for a successful product – that's all that really counts. If a product turns in a profit, after taking into consideration all costs, in perhaps the third year, then they think that they have succeeded. Lessons are learnt very hard – only about 10 per cent of all products that reach the launch stage can be considered successful. In success terms, this means that they still exist after the first year!

To avoid massive spending and possibly massive losses, the business may wish to copy its test launch, but in a different area or segment of the market. Some gradual launches are very popular since costs can be limited and the returns accurately assessed. Advertising and PR can be mobilised to fill in the gaps in public knowledge of the product.

Media planning

There is a very wide choice of media, including over a dozen daily national newspapers, hundreds of regional papers, sixteen independent TV stations, satellite TV, over fifty independent radio stations, over a thousand cinemas, hundreds of weekly and monthly magazines and outdoor advertising opportunities. Quite a choice! Where do you start?

The first two things to think of are:

1 How many of the target audience would you like to get your message through to?
2 How often do you intend to run your advertisements?

These are alternatively known as coverage and frequency. There are several factors which directly relate to this:

- How big is your budget?
- How accurate is your profile of the target market?
- Compare the profile of the media and that of your target – this can be useful in cutting out inappropriate media.
- What is the cost-effectiveness of the media (i.e. CPT or cost per thousand that is reached)?
- How many OTS (opportunities to see) are there with one advertisement?
- Make some rough comparisons between the different media's CPT and OTS.
- Consider the four directions in which your budget and needs are pulling: continuity of advertising (longer-term campaigns), coverage in several different media simultaneously, frequency of your advertising (more slots), and impact (longer individual advertisements, colour advertisements or bigger spaces in printed materials).

A full account of the advantages and disadvantages of each media appears in the companion volume to this book *Marketing In Action*.

Hoseasons Holidays

Hoseasons is a well-established family holiday business which was founded some 47 years ago. It began by offering boating holidays in the UK and for many years this was the mainstay of the business. Now, however, this accounts for only a relatively small part of the turnover – increasingly, it is their self-catering holiday homes which make up the bulk of the holidays they organise.

A relatively recent departure for them has been the establishment of Hoseasons Holidays Abroad. These are also self-catering, and offer a wide range of apartments, cottages and gîtes in France, Germany, Holland, Belgium, Spain and Ireland.

Hoseasons does not own any of the properties. Rather they act as 'marketing agents' for the owners. This also, surprisingly, is true of their original boat business. They call themselves a 'marketing agency' – in fact this is a much better description of what they do. They let the properties on behalf of the owners via their brochures, travel agents and experienced telesales teams. Hoseasons receive a commission on each let they manage to arrange. Hoseasons invest in printing, advertising, staff training and computers; returns are only obtained later, after a successful season.

They provide holidays for a staggering 1 000 000 people in the UK each year. This is broken down into what equates to 250 000 (approx.) holidays with an average of four people going on each holiday. They are the biggest booking agent for holidays in the UK, being twice the size of their biggest competitor, Blakes. Individually, they account for some 50 per cent of all boating holidays and handle some 8500 properties in the UK and Europe for clients. The majority of UK-based holidays are in caravans, lodges, holiday parks and villages.

They employ some 200 staff at the headquarters (currently based in Oulton Broad, Suffolk, although they are due to move by the time of

HOSEASONS
The Best
BOATING IN BRITAIN

NORFOLK BROADS
THAMES VALLEY AND CAMBRIDGESHIRE
CANALS AND RIVERS OF ENGLAND AND WALES
SCOTLAND'S LOCHS

FOUR TIMES WINNERS
Travel Trades'
'BEST OPERATOR – HOLIDAYS AFLOAT' Award

Britain's most modern hire fleet – Over 160 New Boats since 1990

Fig 21
The imagery of a holiday company's brochure is critical in attracting the attention of customers, even with a company as well known as Hoseasons.

publication of this book to Lowestoft, Suffolk). The staff are mainly in the bookings area, and all are excellently trained – indeed their training programmes have won several industry awards. They plan to answer every call within three rings – quite a feat in busy periods! All sales staff are taken to see the properties on offer. This has proved to be a valuable asset in the cross-selling of properties, i.e. if the chosen property is booked for the period required, then the sales person can re-direct the customer to a similar property that they have personal knowledge of. They have very good staff/management relations which has the twofold advantage of low staff turnover and high staff knowledge and commitment to the business.

ADVERTISING AND MARKETING . . . .

We interviewed Hoseasons' new Marketing Manager, Alan Hopley, who came to the company in 1991 from London Underground. He describes himself as 'classically trained', in other words he has a wide range of good qualifications in the marketing field and is extremely up to date with modern methods of marketing. Hoseasons itself is a traditional-style company, certainly as far as marketing is concerned, with a reputation of being 'solid', a 'family business' and 'dependable'. They certainly favoured evolution and not revolution in their marketing and general business strategies.

Having said this, they were real innovators in the direct marketing side of the business. Setting up the brochure/telebookings method of holiday sales several years ago put them well ahead of the competition.

Their advertising and marketing effort is multi-faceted. Here are the main components of their strategies and tactics:

1 **Press advertising** This consists of small display advertisements in the classified sections of newspapers and magazines. These are direct response advertisements to order brochures. Hoseasons put a reference number on each of the advertisements so that they can easily work out how effective the advertisement has been in a particular newspaper or magazine. The reference stays with the customer's name and address on the database, it is printed on the brochure that is sent to them and remains with them right up to the actual booking of the holiday. Hoseasons can amass very useful information known as 'conversion rates', that is how many brochures need to be sent out to get one booking, target areas, selected newspapers and size of advertisements.

2 **TV advertising** is not really cost-effective for Hoseasons, but this is undertaken as a direct response mechanism, mainly to increase and maintain brand awareness of Hoseasons.

3 **Advertising and promotions aimed at the travel agent** Hoseasons have a range of appointed agents throughout the UK. It is a very

competitive market even in terms of getting your brochure on display in the shop. This is a big growth area and now accounts for some 50 per cent of the business.

4 **Magazines** These feature the display/classified advertisement and occasionally full-page advertisements for brand name awareness purposes. Women's magazines, holiday magazines, TV listing and TV Guide magazines, and *Dalton's Weekly* are favoured publications.

Fig 22
Different brochures are produced for different markets.

Fig 23
Another example of the Hoseasons range.

5 **National newspapers** These split into various different categories, which mirror the four main 'product lines' which Hoseasons offer:

a **Hoseasons Holidays** (UK chalets/cottages/lodges/caravans) – mainly for the B/C1/C2 social classes. Good media for this category are the *Daily Mail*, *Daily Mirror* and *Mail On Sunday*.

b **Hoseasons Boating** (UK Norfolk Broads/Thames Valley/ Cambridgeshire/Canals/Scottish Lochs) – mainly for B social class, and again the same kind of newspapers show good responses.

    c **Hoseasons Abroad** (gîtes/cottages/villas) and **Hoseasons Boating in France and Holland** (most of France and Friesland, Holland) – cater for A/B social classes. Hoseasons find that *The Observer* and *The Times* are the best media for this type of holiday.

6 **Radio and TV Times** – are good for Hoseasons. Their campaign starts in November with the distribution of new brochures, as the traditional booking season is January–March for the summer.

Hoseasons place a staggering 1800 plus advertisements in various newspapers and magazines each year. This means that there is a high administrative cost to pay in making sure that all the advertisements are worth placing. For the bulk of the advertisements Alan recognises that there is little opportunity for creativity. This is perhaps a good point in the discussion to look at exactly what he does do:

1 He decides who will receive the 3 000 000 brochures printed every year, what quantities are asked for and the number of enquiries and bookings which these generate.
2 He is responsible for booking advertising space and making sure that the copy arrives with the publication on time.
3 He continually assesses the strengths and weaknesses of the marketing strategy, offering suggestions for improvement and streamlining.
4 He looks at profitability and tries to work out areas of potential growth. This is directly related to 3 above.
5 He painstakingly assesses last year's performance figures and amends plans in relation to those figures.
6 He comes up with new ways of selling existing 'product lines' and looks at the comparative costs.
7 He assesses the relative effectiveness and conversion rates of different elements of Hoseasons (i.e. travel agents vs. telesales etc.).

Alan sees Hoseasons as being a very market-orientated company. They move with the times and recognise that 'product lines' offered five years ago are not necessarily relevant to the customers that they are attracting now.

HE TRAVEL TRADE CAMPAIGN . . . .

Alan works closely with Hoseasons' Travel Trade Sales Manager who uses his marketing and advertising support. As we have already mentioned, the travel agent side of the business is growing rapidly as a percentage of their total turnover. In order to keep abreast with this growth and try to gain a bigger slice of the market it was felt that a specific campaign should be launched in this area.

Normal bookings via the direct response advertising and the telesales department are made, in the main, around the first three months of the year. Travel agent sales are made later, usually clustered around the March to May period. In order to ensure these bookings, Hoseasons support the travel agent in the following ways:

1 They supply a marketing booklet and file on the company, providing information usable by the travel agent's staff. This has a twofold purpose, first to get the travel agent to put their brochures on the shelves, and secondly to encourage the agents to recommend Hoseasons' holidays to their clients.

2 They make sure that sales representatives visit to help reinforce the agent's awareness of Hoseasons. Reps carry a stock of brochures and ready-made window displays that they will fit for the agents! Two sales representatives continually tour the country visiting agents all year round.

3 Hoseasons also provides Prestel and Viewdata details to ease the burden on travel agents.

Hoseasons' database of many thousands of past customers is the first point of reference in any mailshot of brochures each year.

Some travel agents do not work out for Hoseasons. Since the cost of each of the brochures is £1 or thereabouts, it is a considerable cost to them if the brochures are given away without getting back a good return in terms of bookings. If an agent has several hundred brochures, Hoseasons needs and expects a good level of bookings.

Returning to the campaign itself, Hoseasons run a series of full-page colour advertisements telling agents exactly what Hoseasons can offer them. This is part of a continual campaign, seen as important for the following reasons:

1 Travel agents have a high turnover of staff, hence Hoseasons' need continually to repeat themselves.

2 Hoseasons have no direct control over the bookings, so it is important to get the travel agents on their side.

3 The competition is always running advertisements and campaigns, so it makes sense for Hoseasons to keep up in terms of exposure.

4 Regular mailshots to the travel agents keep them in touch with the company and serve as a constant reminder.

5 Marketing packs, a continual stream of leaflets, electronic messages, 'phone calls, prizes and competitions all help to promote the company.

HOSEASONS AND THE FUTURE . . . .

Finally, we asked Alan about the future. Obviously he couldn't tell us anything sensitive, but we asked him why he thinks Hoseasons have diversified the way they have and why they market their services the way they do. His replies are summarised as follows:

1 The boat business has a finite demand. Indeed there is a maximum capacity, hence it is not an ever-expanding market.

2 They wanted to maintain quality. They could have expanded in the boat business, but this would have meant using poorer quality boats.

3 The self-catering business is a little like a 'static boat'. Hoseasons has no knowledge of the hotel business or how to organise package tours. This is, however, an expanding market with enormous growth potential, and so is under constant review.

4 The Hoseasons Abroad was a natural development – they already had the expertise and could easily transfer this knowledge across national boundaries.

5 Hoseasons do not discount their holidays – it is a company policy. They have never, nor ever will. Margins are tight enough being booking agents and as the quality is assured, the price must be maintained.

ACTIVITIES AND TASKS . . . .

1 In the role of Alan, devise a marketing plan for a brochure featuring self-catering holidays in the USA. You should profile your target customers and identify newspapers and magazines which would be suitable for direct response advertising.

2 Again in the role of Alan, devise a sales support pack for travel agents which features details about the company and the new self-catering holidays in the USA.

3 In the role of Hoseasons Travel Trade Sales Manager, prepare a brief presentation to the sales representatives and a group of travel agents about the company and the new holidays.

4 Hoseasons' name is linked closely to boating holidays; however, this is a limited market. In the role of Alan, devise a cheap and effective marketing strategy to 're-educate' the public about Hoseasons' alternative holidays.

THE THEORY BEHIND IT ALL

For this case study we thought it a good idea to look at the role of the marketing manager or director so that you can compare the theory with the reality of Alan's job. In particular, we will also look at the nature of a market-orientated organisation.

The role of the marketing manager

Managers, and in particular marketing managers, are responsible for the planning, organising, controlling and directing of the marketing effort of the company.

Planning plays an essential role in all of this. The marketing manager has to set a number of objectives and think about how he or she can implement them. How these objectives are arrived at depends very much on the nature of the business, but here are some rough guidelines:

- Through analysis of performance, both current and past, of all products.
- Through a review of the marketing opportunities and possible threats to these opportunities.
- Through relating these plans to the overall corporate objectives.

Once these have been established, the manager must decide on the route that should be taken to achieve these objectives. These decisions should always include the following:

- The selection of the marketing targets
- Market positioning
- An appropriate marketing mix.

On the subject of the marketing mix, let's look at the main considerations that should make up the mix:

1 **Strategic considerations** What should we produce and how can we satisfy demands?

2 Tactical considerations How can we get the message across?

3 Planning considerations What is the company's long-term aims?

4 Resource considerations How much can we afford in the promotion of the product and for how long?

5 Operational considerations Can we do it all ourselves?

As you will no doubt remember, the marketing mix aims to do the following:

1 Make sure the price is right.
2 Make sure that you have made or are offering the right product or service.
3 Make sure it is available widely.
4 Make sure that it is there when needed.

The market-orientated organisation

A market-orientated organisation looks at the sales process like this:

1 What do people want?
2 How many do they want?
3 How much will they pay?
4 Can we make a profit?
5 If we can, we'll make what they want.

The organisation is geared to the needs of the customer – it notes and asks about quality, reliability and price. This can often mean that companies have to radically change their nature to be market-orientated. Ideally, they should consider the following key features of marketing:

● Focus the attention of the company on what the customer wants.
● Define specific targets to satisfy – this makes the job easier.
● Make decisions in the company in relation to the customer, always.
● Customer satisfaction is the key to business success.
● A good idea is useless without a viable plan of implementation.
● You must analyse the market, analyse the sales figures, analyse everything!
● Marketing is like a philosophy, it should permeate all of your thinking.
● You may need to reorganise to make things work.
● Be ready to adopt new techniques and ideas.

Cosmetics To Go

Cosmetics To Go is the mail-order cosmetics subsidiary of Constantine and Weir (Mark Constantine and Liz Weir being the original directors). They have been manufacturing cosmetics and beauty products for some fifteen years.

Mark Constantine, a member of the Institute of Trichologists, began his working life, as did Liz Weir, as a health and beauty therapist. Their hair treatment business was based on their abiding interest in herbalism. Even at this early stage they produced their own products These naturally produced lotions, although being both environmentally friendly and not tested on animals, were not appealing to the public, as they discovered. Some were authentic, old remedies that had been used for centuries, but ultimately were boring despite their effectiveness. They lacked impact visually and desperately needed a 'new' image. What was needed was a new approach, a new and modern image to capture the imagination of the public. Neither of the directors had a marketing background in the formal sense, but they summed up their attitude and approach by saying that 'obsession was our qualification' and 'we knew *how* to sell.'

Mark Constantine and Liz Weir were both friends of Anita Roddick, who at that time was in the throes of establishing The Body Shop. They linked up with her very early on in the development of The Body Shop concept. Anita shared their enthusiasm and belief in herbal remedies, natural ingredients and non-animal testing. As The Body Shop grew, so too did Constantine and Weir. Not only did they produce the bulk of The Body Shop range, but they also invented and developed many of them too.

Rowena Hofbauer joined Constantine and Weir, later becoming co-director, at a time when expansion and diversification was needed. She is credited with coming up with the idea of calling their fledglin mail-order cosmetics retailing business Cosmetics To Go. On a visit

ig 24
owena Hofbauer

to Habitat she spotted the phrase 'Divans To Go' – it was as simple as that. The name originally intended for the new business was 'Cosmetic Arts' and the mail-order business had in fact been registered as that. It was, however, changed very quickly.

In terms of style and design, Cosmetics To Go uses predominantly yellow and blue, always attempting to attain a strikingly bold image. The Cosmetics To Go logo itself was designed so that the centre could be replaced with different brand names and messages.

Mark, Liz and Rowena set out a number of guidelines right from the beginning, although they freely admit that they have not always stuck to them. They were:

1 Since this was to be a mail-order business only (they have subsequently set up a shop under their head office in Poole), the catalogues would have to be their main selling vehicle.
2 All products would be illustrated full-size in the catalogues to show the customer exactly what they were getting for their money.
3 All the products would have a background story which would help explain the product and give a little detail about the ingredients.
4 They wanted to exude knowledge and show the customer that the company really understood the product and its abilities. The

directors all agree that their strongest advantage was a very good product knowledge.

5 The mail-order service should be excellent, both in terms of efficiency and courtesy.

6 All products should carry a full listing of the ingredients.

Since the average Cosmetics To Go order is only £12, the need for customer satisfaction is high so as to build up loyalty to the company. They quickly respond to requests and always try to make the arrival of a Cosmetics To Go package exciting for the customer. To this end they invariably put in small gifts, decorate the box with a variety of stickers (from 'How to make a water bomb' to seasonal messages), and use brightly coloured packing materials.

Personal recommendations are the life-blood of the company, and they recognise this as the key to their success. They back up their mail-order business with Roadshows which visit various locations around the country. The 1991 tour included Bournemouth, Bath, Edinburgh and Oxford.

Their new catalogue (of which a page is illustrated in Fig 25) was the result of a 7500-respondent questionnaire. They completed a very full and complex analysis of the questionnaire and made changes accordingly to systems, product lines and policies.

Cosmetics To Go produces two main catalogues a year, in August and in March, backed up by two 'specials'. These are basically seasonal catalogues, arriving with the customers in the summer and in early October ready for Christmas. In their fourth year of mail-order Cosmetics To Go are quite rightly proud of their 55 per cent reorder rate from customers and their ever-improving service is best summed in two quotes, the first from Mark Constantine:

'Every customer counts. You have to do what's best for your customers.'

Rowena Hofbauer goes on to say:

'Because mail-order is thousands of names, you can lose your courtesy with one – we don't aim to ever do that.'

It seems to be paying off. Some 75 people work for the group as a whole. They employ full-time consultants and specialists, who concentrate on ingredients, ideas and animal test monitoring (to keep abreast of the situation and avoid using products so tested). Interestingly, they only promote people to higher positions in the business from within, and never take on staff to posts of authority from outside the company. This has meant that staff loyalty is second to none.

We asked Mark Constantine one final, general question: who did he see as Cosmetics To Go's main competitor? He answered immediately and absolutely truthfully – 'Avon'. Ambitious? Perhaps, but complacent companies are often knocked off their perches by energetic newcomers!

THE S.W.A.L.K. RANGE CREATION AND CAMPAIGN . . . .

S.W.A.L.K. (using the old acronym for 'sealed with a loving kiss') was a major product line release for Cosmetics To Go in 1991. As with many companies, Cosmetics To Go has devised a total product line image to encompass all of the products in the line and provide a base for products to be added at a later date.

Each particular product line has its own identity, and S.W.A.L.K. is no exception to this rule. As you can see from the illustrations, there were some basic guidelines that the directors laid down with regard to product identity throughout their entire product range and these have been rigorously adhered to:

1 Each product is clearly labelled.
2 Each product has a distinct logo of its own.
3 Each product's identity is linged to the overall product line identity.

S.W.A.L.K. is a stand-alone, full-range selection of basic cosmetics and beauty aids consisting of:

- Toothpaste – Kistya.
- Hair wash – Eggo.
- Hair colouring – Dimestore Blonde.
- Eyebrow colour – Hi-brow.
- Foundation powder – Hey Presto.
- Bubble bath – Honey Buns.
- Eye-liner – Goop.
- Hair gel – Pliant Hair Fix.
- Eau de Parfum – Swelegant.
- Lipstick – Luscious, Delicious and Capricious.
- Deodorant – Go For It.

CtoG

PRESENTS

Mistress's Lipstick ✓

FORCES favourites

Ref. No. BFPO2
£3.25
3.5g

istresss Lipstick

When you want to steal a secret kiss or two, lipstick can give the game away. Not so with Mistress's. A bright red lip stain to wear on its own or under your favourite colour. Won't smear, smudge or bleed. Stays put.

Mistress's Lipstick
The ingredients in this product
are *(greatest first)*:
Water, Calcium Sulphate *base*,
F.D. & C. No. 7 *red colour*, F.D. & C.
No. 21 *red colour*, Laneth 40 *moisturising
agent*, Methylparaben *preservative*.

COSMETICS · TO · GO

S.W.A.L.K.

Swelegant - Eau De Parfum ✓

Sandalwood, ylang ylang and clove essential oils blended with violet leaf absolute are the basis of this 'oh, so elegant' fragrance. A highly green, floral scent for every occasion. Dab a little behind your ears and stride forward confidently.

Swelegant
Ylang Ylang, Clove,
Sandalwood, Violet Leaf
Absolute.

Swelegant
EAU DE PARFUM

Ref. No. SW11
£12.75
75ml

Swelegant
EAU DE PARFUM
75ml

Kistya - Toothpaste

Most toothpastes contain Sodium Lauryl Sulphate, a vegetable shampoo base. This gives lots of foam and we use it in our shampoos for that very purpose, but in a toothpaste it can leave the mouth dry and cracked around the corners - nasty ! Therefore, we don't include it in Kistya's 'non-foaming' formula. Our testers found their breath stayed fresher for longer when they tried Kistya. Go on - improve your kissability !

Ref. No. SW1
£2.75
40ml

KISTYA

Kistya
The ingredients
in this product are
(greatest first): Dicalcium
Phosphate Dihydrate *abrasive*,
Water, Glycerin *humectant*,
Carageenan *seaweed for binding*, Sodium
Monoflourophosphate *reputed to have anti
decaying properties*, Sanqui *Chinese herb said to have
anti decaying properties*, Honey *sweetener*, Methylparaben
preservative, Tea Tree essential oil, Eucalyptus essential oil,
Peppermint essential oil, Cognac essential oil, Lime essential oil,
Vanilla essential oil, Otto of Rose. pH6.7

18

Fig 25 (opposite)
A page from the
catalogue: the 1950s
kitsch humour is
central to the
marketing strategy for
the company's SWALK
range.

- Hair grease – Brilliantine.
- Eye shadow – Jolly Roger and Matt Bianco.
- Soap – Complexion.

The central identity for these products is, as you can see, firmly rooted in the 1950s. What made Cosmetics to Go decide to choose this image? Did the product names come first, or did the central identity dictate the names? Why did they decide to launch the range as a whole and not simply incorporate them into another, existing range?

Let's look at these questions in turn. Cosmetics To Go wanted a strong central image or identity for the range. Mark Constantine has a great affinity with the 1950s, enjoying the style and the 'fun' aspects of some of the more inappropriate and odd names given to products in that time. Not content with producing a range of lipsticks and calling them 'red lipstick', or 'pink lipstick', he followed his basic philosophy of clear product identity. Each of the names given to the products have a 1950s 'feel' about them, and they have all been created with that in mind.

It was the need for a new product line that grew first. The identity evolved once the basic decision had been made about the style that was to be employed to market them. Each of the products themselves are simply alternatives to existing ranges that Cosmetics To Go offer. What makes them different is their new, clear and 'corporate-type' style.

Cosmetics To Go take a very pragmatic view about their products. Essentially, if it does not sell, it is dropped, or more accurately phased out of production. You will recall their extensive questionnaire that was undertaken recently and mentioned above. Some products, on a strictly profit-making or turnover basis, had been marked to be dropped by the company. Certain comments and suggestions from their respondents changed the company's opinion, or at least amended it. It was clear that if they did drop some products they would upset regular users. Cosmetics To Go decided on a compromise – these products would either remain, or be adapted and incorporated into another range. A couple of the S.W.A.L.K. products are variants of these, others have been dropped and more have been kept on, pending close inspection of their sales.

It was therefore interesting to consider Cosmetics To Go's attitude to

ORDERING BY POST

ORDERED BY: *(PLEASE USE CAPITAL LETTERS)*

Name _____

Address _____

_____

_____ Post Code _____

Telephone No. _____

Gift card message if any _____

_____

DELIVER TO: *(if different from order address)*

Name _____

Address _____

_____ Post Code _____

Have you ordered from us before? ☐ YES ☐ NO

Ref No.	Description	Qty.	PRICE OF ITEMS	
			Each	Total

FREE Postage in UK only.
Other EC Countries. Please add £4.00.
Countries outside the EC. Please add £7.00   **TOTAL**

METHOD OF PAYMENT

NO CASH PLEASE

☐ CHEQUE OR POSTAL ORDER ENCLOSED (Payable to: Cosmetics • To • Go)

☐ VISA ☐ ACCESS ☐ DINERS CLUB ☐ AMERICAN EXPRESS

EXPIRY DATE: *Month/Year*   SIGNATURE

GUARANTEED to satisfy as much as mere material goods can. If for any reason you are not satisfied with your products please send them back for a refund or exchange. Cosmetics To Go is a trading style of Constantine & Weir Plc Company Registration No. 1619480

COSMETICS • TO • GO,
FREEPOST, Poole Dorset. BH15 1BR

ORDERING BY POST

ORDERED BY: *(PLEASE USE CAPITAL LETTERS)*

Name _____

Address _____

_____

_____ Post Code _____

Telephone No. _____

Gift card message if any _____

_____

DELIVER TO: *(if different from order address)*

Name _____

Address _____

_____ Post Code _____

Have you ordered from us before? ☐ YES ☐ NO

Ref No.	Description	Qty.	PRICE OF ITEMS	
			Each	Total

FREE Postage in UK only.
Other EC Countries. Please add £4.00.
Countries outside the EC. Please add £7.00   **TOTAL**

METHOD OF PAYMENT

NO CASH PLEASE

☐ CHEQUE OR POSTAL ORDER ENCLOSED (Payable to: Cosmetics • To • Go)

☐ VISA ☐ ACCESS ☐ DINERS CLUB ☐ AMERICAN EXPRESS

EXPIRY DATE: *Month/Year*   SIGNATURE

GUARANTEED to satisfy as much as mere material goods can. If for any reason you are not satisfied with your products please send them back for a refund or exchange. Cosmetics To Go is a trading style of Constantine & Weir Plc Company Registration No. 1619480

COSMETICS • TO • GO,
FREEPOST, Poole Dorset. BH15 1BR

Fig 26 (opposite)
A concise, simply-
presented order form is
essential.

the failure of a whole product line. What would they do if
S.W.A.L.K. failed? The initial reaction was to discontinue the line,
but from experience they recognise the unlikely scenario of every
product in the line being a failure equally – some products would be
popular, others not. The latter would be dealt with in the normal
way, being replaced with alternatives, but the product line would
survive. In this way, the range's overall identity would be safe
despite the failure of a product within that range.

The creation of a new product line is a natural evolution of their
overall policy. Many of the products, with specific qualities to offer
the customer, did not fit into any of the existing lines. Rather than
force the product into a range that it was not suited for, diversifying
into another styled range is a logical choice.

Turning to the style of the catalogue, pack design and use of
language, the authentic 1950s approach has been scrupulously
followed. With the advantages of 'copying' a style, Cosmetics To Go
had distinctive guidelines to try to follow.

The pack designs are very 1950s, particularly the logos on the
product and product pack – they are not as clear and bold as we
would expect on modern products. Notice too how many of the
products bear an 'old-fashioned', 'hand-written' quality to their
logos. This is very reminiscent of the 1950s.

The text has a 'tongue-in-cheek' approach. Take Swelegant as an
example:

> You can always afford to buy . . .
>
> **Swelegant**
>
> – oh, so elegant!
>
> *What every housewife really wants*
> A delightfully cheerful new fragrance for all occasions. Even a poem
> couldn't describe the beguiling smell of sweet violets and ylang flowers.
>
> You owe it to yourself – to him – to keep glamorous.
>
> Feel it, sense it, as depression flies away when you wear Swelegant.
>
> *Who knows whose nose knows best?*
>
> A pleasure to get and even better to give.
> Have you tried it yet?

The effect is very corny – and meant to be. An advertiser without setting up the background for a product like this would not get away with saying this. The range's identity allows this approach: it is in the style of 1950s' advertisements and the reader is well aware of this. The approach can then be humorous and readers will not think that it is just terrible! Or offensive to feminists even?

With regard to the catalogue, putting aside the style of the text and advertising genre, the message is still clear to the customer. They are left in no doubt as to the nature of the product, the effects, the advantages and the look that you can achieve by using it. Cosmetics To Go have deviated from one of their major philosophies – the products are not displayed in their true size – but each product is clearly marked as to the weight or volume in each case.

S.W.A.L.K. has proved to be a resounding success, and new products are being added immediately while others are in the pipeline. The advantages of a clear image has paid off. Customers like the style and enjoy being able to use a whole range with a clear, standard identity. The jokey text style is in line with the rest of their product ranges. Cosmetics To Go try to get over the concept that the products are fun – their existing customers accept this approach and have come to expect it too. New customers are quickly socialised into this attitude and welcome this alternative way of describing the products.

ACTIVITIES AND TASKS . . . .

1 In the role of CTG, create your own cosmetics range in their style.
2 Create a short mail-order catalogue for a range of products of your choice. Think of alternative ways of getting your message across. Think about customer loyalty and overall range image.
3 In the role of Mark, Liz and Rowena prepare a marketing plan to develop their range of activities into a new, but related, sphere of operations. You should prepare this with a view to attracting venture capital from outside the company.

THE THEORY BEHIND IT ALL . . . .

Cosmetics To Go brings up a number of interesting theoretical approaches to marketing. Let's look at them in a little detail.

Product planning

1 Proactive product planning can be a somewhat tricky and dangerous policy to undertake. It involves creating a brand new product for which there is not a fully tested and established market. Cosmetics To Go follow this policy line. This is the opposite of the more conservative reactive policy that simply follows the trends and mimics a more established product with a 'new' version.

2 Key considerations regarding the development of a new product include the following:
a Does the product meet the needs of the target market?
b Does the product have any advantages in terms of design, reliability or quality?
c Does the product stand up to the demands that will be made of it?
d Does it match up with or add to the target's self-image?
e Does the product match up well against the opposition?
f Does the product have the right image and presentation?
g Does it cost less than the competition?
h Does the product offer a good profit margin?
i Is it possible to maintain a consistent standard of product?

Direct marketing – mail-order and maintaining customer loyalty

Mail-order is the most common and well-developed form of direct marketing. It often relies on a catalogue which describes the product and its price, availability and how to order it. The catalogue is the main selling vehicle, so it needs to reflect a number of things which have a direct impact on the reorder rate of the customer:

1 It must be easy to find the product you need.
2 It must be easy to reorder (an 0800 number is quoted as an alternative to postal orders by Cosmetics To Go).
3 The catalogue should reflect the needs, attitudes and interests of the customers.
4 The catalogue should readily be 'changeable' under pressure from the expressed needs of the customers.

As regards customer loyalty, several levels have been identified as follows:

1 **Hard-core loyalty** total commitment by consumers (very rare).

2 **Soft-core loyalty** divided loyalty – consumers may shift from a selection of two or three brands (much more common).

3 **Shifting** pattern of constant change to and from a range of products (very common).

4 **Switching** consumers have no real loyalty to any product or company. They are heavily influenced by special offers and promotions.

Cosmetics To Go have a foundation of customers in the hard-core category, though most fall in the soft-core category in terms of loyalty. They occasionally attract customers from the other two categories, as do many other companies. The trick is to turn these customers into one of the first two categories, and Cosmetics To Go have a definite policy aimed at this conversion. Most other mail-order businesses have similar policies for retaining their customers whatever their reorder rate.

Lynx

Lynx was founded in November 1985 by Mark Glover, an ex-member of Greenpeace. With a background in pure science, Mark had a long standing interest in natural history which, since the 1970s, had been compounded with a growing fear of the consequences of the way man is treating the earth and its creatures. Whilst studying for his doctorate he was offered the job of wildlife campaigner at Greenpeace.

During his four and a half years at Greenpeace, Mark worked on the whale and seal campaigns amongst others, as well as on the fur issue. As he saw it the latter showed in no uncertain terms the political and commercial exploitation involved. At the end of 1985, Mark left Greenpeace and formed Lynx – an organisation devoted to combating the 'cruel and unnecessary' fur trade.

Lynx is a very vigorous and high-profile charity. In a relatively short time (perhaps aided to some extent by the recession, as critics would claim) it has achieved remarkable successes. Their first major campaign *Dumb Animals*, featuring the photography of David Bailey, was launched in the winter of 1986. This culminated in the Lynx Round Britain Tour that year. The following year saw the launch of the *Fashion Accessories* poster and the *Scavengers* cinema advertisement. By 1987, Lynx had established through market research that 70 per cent of the public believed that it was wrong to kill animals for their fur.

An independent Gallup poll in October 1988 backed up their findings putting the figure at 85 per cent. This coincided with the opening of the first Lynx shop in Covent Garden the following month. There was even better news for them that month – Edelson Furs, a company with a previous turnover of some £20 million, had called in the receivers.

In January 1989 the Lynx *Roar of Disapproval* video was released.

THE TRAPPER APPROACHED , A FIVE FOOT GREEN BIRCH CLUB IN HAND. THE COYOTE STRUGGLED FRANTICALLY AGAINST THE TRAP, PULLING ONE LEG LOOSE AND LEAVING THE LIFELESS PAW IN THE TRAP. THE TRAPPER POKED AT THE COYOTE. THE ANIMAL HISSED AND SNAPPED AT THE CLUB. THEN, AS THE TRAPPER SLOWLY SWISHED THE CLUB BACK AND FORTH, THE COYOTE BECAME UNUSUALLY CALM. MESMERISED BY STEADY MOTION, HE CROUCHED MOTIONLESS, HIS EYES DUTIFULLY FOLLOWING THE SWISHING CLUB SUDDENLY THE CLUB SMASHED ACROSS THE COYOTE'S NOSE AND SLAMMED HIM TO THE GROUND. BUT THE BLOW WAS NOT DELIVERED WITH PRECISION. ALMOST INSTANTLY HE WAS IN A SEMI -CROUCH; BLOOD SPURTING FROM HIS NOSE, EYES DAZED. AGAIN THE CLUB FELL. THE TRAPPER, IN ONE PRACTISED MOTION, GRABBED THE STUNNED COYOTE BY THE HIND LEGS, STRETCHING THE ANIMAL FULL LENGTH WHILE PLANTING HIS FOOT HEAVILY ON ITS NECK.

THE OTHER FOOT DELIVERED A SERIES OF THUMPING BLOWS TO THE COYOTES CHEST, EXPELLING HOLLOW GASPS OF AIR. RELEASING THE HIND LEGS, THE TRAPPER RESTED ONE FOOT ON THE COYOTE 'S NECK, THE OTHER ON THE CHEST. THE COYOTE'S EYES BULGED, THE MOUTH GAPED, THE TONGUE HUNG LISTLESSLY ALONG THE BLOODSTAINED JAW. PERIODICALLY STOMPING NEAR THE HEART, THE TRAPPER MAINTAINED HIS POSITION FOR 14 MINUTES. HE INDICATED THIS WAS NECESSARY TO ENSURE THAT THE ANIMAL WAS DEAD-"ONCE I HAD ONE LEAP UP AND TAKE A BITE AT ME". WHILE FOCUSSING THE CAMERA, I THOUGHT HOW RIDICULOUS IT WAS FOR A 200 POUND MAN TO BE STOMPING ON AN 18 POUND COYOTE AS IF HIS VERY EXISTENCE DEPENDED ON THE ANIMAL'S ELIMINATION. THE COYOTE, HAD HE BEEN GIVEN THE OPPORTUNITY, WOULD NOT EVEN HAVE SOUGHT REVENGE. HE WOULD HAVE TRIED TO ESCAPE '

Each year more than 300,000 coyotes are amongst the 20 million wild animals trapped and killed for their fur

Fig 27
A page from a Lynx brochure – Lynx has now become famed for its striking and brutal imagery.

That month also saw the first counter-demonstration by fur traders outside the Lynx shop in London.

In fact 1989 was to be one of the best years for the organisation. In March Konrads, one of the West End's leading furriers, appointed receivers as Lynx swung several new campaigns into action. In August they announced their *Fur Amnesty Tour*, which offered fur product owners the opportunity to hand in their furs to Lynx for disposal. In October Lynx launched the *Rich Bitch, Poor Bitch* poster campaign, photographed by Linda McCartney (more details are given below). This campaign was also supported by a major rally in Trafalgar Square.

October also saw the closure of Hudsons Bay after 319 years of fur trading in the Pool of London. The company was originally founded under royal charter granted by Charles II in 1670.

In late November Lynx launched their fashion show at the Waldorf Hotel and announced the opening of their second shop, this time in Cambridge. Furriers again attempted to demonstrate and disrupt the fashion show.

A National Westminster Bank memorandum was leaked to Lynx in January 1990. It revealed: 'Over twenty furriers ceased trading in 1988.' It went on: 'The value of [fur] goods produced by the UK has declined £78m in four years,' and: 'The sales figures of fur goods have declined by almost 50% since 1986.' Finally: 'Companies are closing down regularly and no producer in this country can really feel secure.'

As if in direct response to the leaked memorandum, Harrods announced the closure of its fur department the following month. (It in fact closed in April.)

Lynx were again on the move, opening an office in the USA in October 1990, launching another fashion show and celebrating its fifth birthday. Selfridges also followed Harrods' lead that November by announcing the closure of their fur department. By December the *Dumb Animals* poster had been unveiled in New York and Los Angeles.

Lynx released its *Fur Factories* video in March 1991, and held a fashion sale in June to help raise funds. The *Mass Fur Coat Burial* was undertaken in August. Lynx's third shop opened in Nottingham in September.

Meanwhile the American campaign was gathering steam. In October Lynx began advertising their new posters in Los Angeles and New York. Elton John, one of their patrons, appeared in a Public Service Announcement supporting Lynx.

Back in the UK, Lynx rounded off the year with two events in November – their new *They're Back* poster campaign and the Lynx

International Fashion Show at the London Hippodrome.

We now turn our attention to one of their major campaigns of recent years, the *Rich Bitch, Poor Bitch* poster. We will also look at the PR and media releases for their *Lynx Mass Fur Burial*.

THE *RICH BITCH, POOR BITCH* CAMPAIGN . . . .

The central image of the poster campaign featured on one side a 'rich bitch' in a glossy fur coat, on the other a 'poor bitch' – the blood-stained corpse of a fox.

The poster was the latest salvo in their campaign against the $6 billion fur trade. 'If you don't want millions of animals tortured or killed in leg traps, don't buy a fur coat.' This was the slogan seen across the length and breadth of the country. The poster was subsequently translated and used in other campaigns around Europe.

Rich bitch.   Poor bitch.

If you don't want millions of animals tortured and killed in leg-hold traps don't buy a fur coat.   **LYNX**

Fig 28
Clever marketing does not have to be subtle – the impact is in the juxtaposition of image and legend.

The poster attracted masses of useful press coverage. Below are some extracts which highlight the key features of the campaign:

Paul McCartney's wife Linda has joined forces with Lynx, the anti-fur organisation to produce a gory, stomach churning poster aimed at deterring people from buying fur coats this Christmas.

Linda's work for Lynx follows a tradition established three years ago by top photographers Clive Aris and David Bailey, who shot the organisation's first two controversial posters.

'Linda McCartney readily accepted our commission to shoot the poster,' said Lynx spokeswoman Lin Kentish. 'She was in complete agreement with our policy of extremely shocking posters. Only forceful advertising will shift old, cruel and outworn attitudes.'

The photograph was staged in a London studio, using a dead fox and took eight hours to set up and shoot.

Linda is expected to turn up with anti-fur trade rock star pals Chrissie Hynes, Kevin Godley and Annie Lennox at a Lynx Bring Out Your Dead rally in London's Trafalgar Square next Saturday.

Daily Express, October 1989

The new billboards will be on display the length and breadth of Britain this coming winter there. Lynx expects to be able to put up three times as many posters than ever in the coming four months, and hopes that the high profile the campaign is bound to achieve will have further effect on the dwindling fur trade. The Yellowhammer advertising agency designed and produced this new piece of work for Lynx.

Buenos Aires Herald, November 1989

Lynx is deliberately targeting the areas traditionally associated with fashion and style – it hopes to raise awareness in Milan, Rome, Paris and Berlin next year.

World Magazine, November 1989

Top model Yasmin Le Bon (the 'rich bitch' on the poster) backs Lynx's aims totally. 'It is barbaric to kill animals for vanity,' she says. 'Fur doesn't keep you any warmer than anything else and there are more glamorous things to wear than dead animals.'

Today, September 1989

Lynx sees it (the fur trade) as 'an industry soaked in blood and gore' and which is close to collapse. It says that fur sales have halved in the past five years and that twenty fur shops went out of business in the past year alone.

The Financial Times, October 1989

There was also some activity from the opposition at this time. *Time Out* featured the script of a radio advertisement from the US Pro-Fur group:

There you are. At a pleasant restaurant, enjoying the conversation and a nice steak dinner. Suddenly there's a commotion. People are around your table jostling you. Shouting. Pointing at your steak and screaming that you are a killer! The animal activists – the same ones who are making such a noise about wearing fur right now – are against the use of animals which involves what they consider 'mistreatment'. That includes everything from the wearing of fur. And leather. Eating meat. Poultry. Even eggs. The use of animals in medical research. Zoos. Circuses. You see, fur is just the beginning for them. The fur industry believes in and is committed to the responsible treatment of animals. But we also believe that the decision to wear or not to wear fur is a personal one. Shouldn't individuals be free from harassment, verbal abuse and violence from animal activists? This is not just a fur industry issue. It's everybody's issue.

Time Out, April 1990

In any event, in the UK such publications as *Elle*, *She*, *Today* and *Cosmopolitan* maintain strict bans on fur advertising and editorial (*Vogue* says it only features farmed furs), although in the US there has been no media boycott.

Mark summed up the success of the campaign when he was asked who wears furs these days: 'I have to be honest, hardly anyone. A large proportion of people wearing fur coats here are foreigners.'

Does he think that the advertising is unnecessarily intimidating? 'I would never use the word intimidation. We are just attempting to shame fur-coat wearers into not wearing fur.'

THE *MASS FUR BURIAL* CAMPAIGN . . . .

We include one of the three major press releases of this campaign to illustrate the activity. It culminated in the burial of thousands of fur garments in Devon in August 1991. (See also pages 110 and 111.)

A couple of points that appear on press releases may need further explanation:

1 **For favour of publication** This means that the sender feels that this item is for general interest and consumption and should have some preferential treatment.
2 **No embargo** This means that the information contained in the press release may be featured in the press immediately. Usually there may be a date before which the press release information remains confidential.

The initial press release covered the end of the campaign in terms of collection of furs; the second publicised the actual burial; and the third thanked people for having given furs for burial. This flow of information is essential and is the life-blood of the pressure group.

**Fig 29
An example of a press
release.**

PRESS RELEASE

NO EMBARGO   29th September 1989

LYNX

LYNX
PO BOX 509
DUNMOW
ESSEX
CM6 1UH

0371 2016
FAX 0371 6380

LYNX LAUNCHES NEW AND CONTROVERSIAL LINDA McCARTNEY ANTI-FUR
BILLBOARD POSTER IN THE MIDLANDS

The first of Lynx's new anti-fur billboard posters that will
form part of a massive new campaign against the fur trade
will be on display in the Midlands region during October.

The graphic new poster, photographed for Lynx by Linda McCartney,
shows a woman reclining wearing a red fox coat with the wording,
in a bold type face - "Rich Bitch". Next to her is a dead
red fox, caught in a leghold trap and surrounded by pools
of blood with the wording "Poor Bitch".

Commenting on the release of the poster, Mark Glover, Lynx
Director said today: "We shall be putting up three times
as many posters this winter than ever before. We hope very
much that this will be one of the last years that we shall
see any fur coats in Britain since the wearing of fur is
both barbaric and outdated".

ENDS

For information regarding the exact location of the Lynx
posters or to obtain either 35mm transparencies or mini proof
versions of the poster please contact the Lynx office.

Posters will be appearing in: BIRMINGHAM, COVENTRY, DUDLEY,
SANDWELL, SOLIHULL, WOLVERHAMPTON, ALFRETON, DERBY, CHELTENHAM,
GLOUCESTER, WORCESTER, LEICESTER, NOTTINGHAM, BURTON UPON
TRENT, STOKE ON TRENT, NUNEATON, RUGBY AND MANSFIELD
during the calendar month of October.

For further information contact: 0371 872016/876434

CTIVITIES AND TASKS • • • • • • • • • • • • • • • • • • •

1 In the role of Mark Glover prepare a press release for the
forthcoming campaign which identifies the companies who own
the fur businesses in the UK. This will be under the title of the
'Dirty Dozen'. You should consider when the information should

be given to the press and format the press release in the
appropriate manner.

2 Lynx places a great deal of value on celebrity endorsements of
their campaign. In the role of the press and public relations
manager for a major superstar (of your choice) how would you
cope with the masses of enquiries and pleas to support various
causes. You should identify a general response with appropriate
'no thank you' and 'would be delighted' letters to suit.

3 Lynx is a pressure group and runs its affairs mainly from the
income derived from donations and membership as well as the
sales of merchandising. In the role of Lynx's merchandising
manager design a full range of merchandising items which will
appeal to a wide range of ages and pockets.

4 The message that Lynx is trying to get across is aimed not only
at the general public, but at a very specific section of the
community – those who can afford furs. Identify a 'hit-list' of
publications which appeal to this market and prepare a press
release in favour of Lynx's stand on the fur issue.

THE THEORY BEHIND IT ALL . . . .

There are two main areas of theory arising from the Lynx case study
first, the uses of outdoor advertising as a favoured medium; secondly
the use of celebrities to endorse products and causes.

Outdoor advertising

Outdoor advertising, in theory, can claim to be the most effective.
Nearly everyone will see a poster if it is well sited (apart from those
living in the middle of nowhere of course!). The average CPT is
around 30p.

Below are some of the advantages and disadvantages of outdoor
advertising. Remember that this category also includes such media as
buses, football stadiums, hot-air balloons, milk bottles and even
parking meters (the authors' absolute favourites!).

Advantages:

● Very high OTS.
● Very low CPT.

- Wide range of colour available.
- Wide range of sites.
- Little direct competition.
- Sites sold on quarterly basis, therefore the viewer can subconsciously notice the advertisement over a long period of time.
- Great opportunities for very innovative and striking advertisements in terms of size and possible 3-D.

Disadvantages:

- Printing costs are high for short print runs of the advertisement.
- There is a long booking and cancellation waiting period.
- There is only basic research on the effectiveness of individual sites.
- Certain sites can be easily missed and not looked at.
- Only short, snappy messages can really be used.
- Graffiti can be a problem.
- Prime sites are often monopolised by big advertisers. They are booked on a TC (till cancelled) basis, so may be booked for years on end.
- Individual sites are not often available on their own – sites are usually rented in a package deal including several different sites.

Celebrity and personality endorsements

Several companies have created fictitious characters which are associated with their products. For example, Mr Wimpey, George the Hoffmeister bear, the Oxo family, the Bisto kids, the Milky Bar Kid, etc. Point-of-sales displays and other advertising material feature these characters and, by association, seek to enhance the customer's awareness of the product range. Celebrity endorsements (like the Lynx case study with Linda McCartney and the Ark case study with the Geldofs) or associations have a similar effect.

These associations usually fall into three main categories:

1 **Free promotional help** Mostly related to charities and causes which the celebrity agrees with.
2 **Paid endorsement** For example, a famous celebrity appears in an advertisement or is quoted as using the product.
3 **Sponsorship** Where a sportsman, for example, wears a certain brand of training shoes in return for free goods and money paid into a trust fund (since British athletes are amateurs).

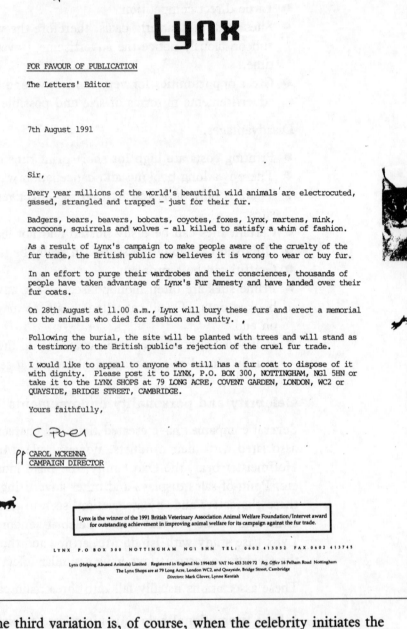

Lynx

FOR FAVOUR OF PUBLICATION

The Letters' Editor

7th August 1991

Sir,

Every year millions of the world's beautiful wild animals are electrocuted, gassed, strangled and trapped - just for their fur.

Badgers, bears, beavers, bobcats, coyotes, foxes, lynx, martens, mink, raccoons, squirrels and wolves - all killed to satisfy a whim of fashion.

As a result of Lynx's campaign to make people aware of the cruelty of the fur trade, the British public now believes it is wrong to wear or buy fur.

In an effort to purge their wardrobes and their consciences, thousands of people have taken advantage of Lynx's Fur Amnesty and have handed over their fur coats.

On 28th August at 11.00 a.m., Lynx will bury these furs and erect a memorial to the animals who died for fashion and vanity.

Following the burial, the site will be planted with trees and will stand as a testimony to the British public's rejection of the cruel fur trade.

I would like to appeal to anyone who still has a fur coat to dispose of it with dignity. Please post it to LYNX, P.O. BOX 300, NOTTINGHAM, NG1 5HN or take it to the LYNX SHOPS at 79 LONG ACRE, COVENT GARDEN, LONDON, WC2 or QUAYSIDE, BRIDGE STREET, CAMBRIDGE.

Yours faithfully,

C Poel

pp CAROL MCKENNA
CAMPAIGN DIRECTOR

Lynx is the winner of the 1991 British Veterinary Association Animal Welfare Foundation/Intervet award for outstanding achievement in improving animal welfare for its campaign against the fur trade.

LYNX P.O BOX 300 NOTTINGHAM NG1 5HN TEL: 0602 413052 FAX 0602 413745

Lynx (Helping Abused Animals) Limited Registered in England No 1994038 VAT No 453 3109 72 *Reg. Office* 16 Pelham Road Nottingham
The Lynx Shops are at 79 Long Acre, London WC2, and Quayside, Bridge Street, Cambridge
Directors: Mark Glover, Lynne Kentish

Fig 30
As well as sending out two Press Releases (see the example on page 106), this Letter was sent out as an alternative campaign strategy.

The third variation is, of course, when the celebrity initiates the product as a business venture. Examples of this are Jane Asher (cookery and cakes, etc.), Linda McCartney (a range of vegetarian convenience foods), Elizabeth Taylor (perfume) and Paul Newman (salad dressing). An interesting development is the BBC's decision to market products using the names of TV chefs, with the BBC logo. These, however, remain rare examples.

Lynx

27 September 1991

To: The Letters Editor

For Favour of Publication

Dear Sir/Madam

I would like to thank all of your readers who supported the recent Lynx Fur Amnesty by sending in their unwanted fur coats.

The mass fur burial took place at an animal sanctuary in South Molton, Devon and a memorial to all the animals who die for fashion was erected.

I am sending a photo of the memorial to assure people who donated furs that their coats were buried as they asked - returning to the earth the remains of the wild creatures which had suffered and died for fashion.

A number of letters appeared in your newspaper from people who were concerned that Lynx had decided to bury the unwanted furs rather than give them to the needy.

I would like to assure those readers that the majority of the furs buried were wholly inappropriate for donating to people in cold, wet or remote areas. They were fashion items: mink jackets, fox stoles and the like which had no practical use and would have become useless very quickly.

There are so many other items, such as food and medicine, which are much more urgently needed. It is for these - and environmental and humane reasons - that so many aid agencies and charity shops no longer accept fur donations.

Yours faithfully

G. Wotherspoon

P.P. Carol McKenna
Campaign Director

Lynx is the winner of the 1991 British Veterinary Association Animal Welfare Foundation/Intervet award
for outstanding achievement in improving animal welfare for its campaign against the fur trade.

LYNX P.O BOX 300 NOTTINGHAM NG1 5HN TEL: 0602 413052 FAX 0602 413745

Lynx (Helping Abused Animals) Limited   Registered in England No 1994038 VAT No 453 3109 72   Reg. Officr 16 Pelham Road Nottingham
The Lynx Shops are at 79 Long Acre, London WC2, and Quayside, Bridge Street, Cambridge
Directors: Mark Glover, Lynne Kentish

**Fig 31
The final press release
of the campaign (see
page 106).**

Glossary of useful terms

Above the line Media advertising, usually aimed at the public.

ACORN A Classification Of Residential Neighbourhoods – classifies people by their housing and assumes similarities.

Added value Associating a product with high quality and good customer service. Making it appear better than the competition.

Advertising One of the techniques of informing the public of your product or service.

After-sales service Making sure that the product performs well after purchase.

Below the line Sales promotions/POS, brochures/mailshots, etc.

BRAD British Rate And Data – a publication giving a listing of media costs.

Brand image The public view of the product.

Brand name The name given to a product to differentiate it from other products.

Branding Giving a product an identity of its own.

Cash cows Products which have reached the mature stage in their product life cycle, bringing in revenue for very little cost.

Competition Defined by the experts as an organisation which produces products that are similar to something that you produce.

Competitors Any rival organisation that may take sales away from you.

Consumer The 'end-user' of the product or service. This may be the manufacturer using your product in their production process, or the customer buying from a retailer.

Consumer market A section of the community who buy products for themselves.

Consumer marketing Marketing aimed specifically at the consumer.

Consumer products Products aimed specifically at the consumer.

Consumer research Research looking into the habits/attitudes/opinions of the consumer.

Consumerism The collective power of the consumer in influencing those who provide the goods and services.

Costing The act of working out mathematically the costs of a product.

Delphi method A panel of experts who are kept apart from each other in order not to be influenced by one another. Used in developing marketing analysis.

Demography The study of population growth, decline and movement.

Design The act of creating an image for a product, service or advertising campaign.

Direct mail Making a sales approach to the customer through the post.

Direct response The attempt to make a customer act immediately.

Discretionary income Money that people have left after all essential spending has been done.

Disposable income Money that people have left after tax and National Insurance payments.

Distribution The process of getting a product or service to the customer, often measured in terms of availability and accessibility.

Dogs Products which have reached the decline period of their life cycle.

Durables Tangible goods that are expected to last some time, like furniture or large electrical goods.

EPOS Electronic Point of Sales – a computerised system that reads the bar code on a product and prints out price and name on a till receipt, and assists reorders.

Exhibitions Demonstrations of the goods or service direct to the public or the business/retail trade. Not always a selling situation.

Field research Collecting 'first-hand' information from the consumer market.

Fixed costs Costs which remain static whatever the level of production or sales.

Franchising Usually a relationship set up where the franchisor provides merchandise/management help and promotional help in return for the franchisee agreeing to buy just from the franchisor and passing across a percentage of the sales.

GDP Gross Domestic Product – total of people's earnings within a country.

Generic A particular product type. Tea is a generic product, but PG Tips is not – it is a brand.

GNP Gross National Product – total of country's earnings.

Hard sell Pressurised selling direct to the consumer.

Image The design created for a product or service, and the message given to the consumer about a product or organisation.

Industrial marketing Marketing directed specifically at the business or industrial sector.

Inflation A financial situation where costs and prices rise and money value decreases, which erodes the purchasing power of businesses and customers alike.

Loss leader A product offered at a loss-making price, for example to attract customers to a shop.

Marginal costing Policy that attempts to cover the variable costs together with a contribution to the overheads.

Market A group of individuals or organisations who are potential buyers.

Market leader The pre-eminent product or service in a market.

Market research Usually refers to research about customers, competitors and markets, etc.

Market segmentation The process of breaking down markets into groups that might usefully be targeted.

Marketing Supplying customers with what they want, when and where they want it, at a price that both satisfies them and provides a profit.

Marketing mix Combining marketing methods to achieve profitable exploration of the market.

Marketing research The use of scientific methods to collect information about customers, competitors and markets, etc.

Merchandising Part of sales promotion aimed at generating the customer's interest in a product or service.

Middlemen People or organisations which handle distribution of the manufacturer's goods or services to the customer.

Motivation The generation of, or the existence of, the desire to do something.

Non-durables Tangible goods that are often used up quickly, like food for example.

Organisational market A market where the customer is a business organisation, or a manufacturer using the product in the production of other products (eg raw materials).

Panels Groups of consumers who record their purchases.

Perceived quality A customer has a tendency to associate a high price with high quality. The quality may not necessarily be inherent, but the manufacturer still charges a high price.

PEST Political, Economic, Social and Technological factors which make up the external environment that can influence an organisation.

Point of sale (POS) Displays, posters, racks, signs, etc, by or near the product in a shop.

Positioning The way a product or service is seen in relation to competing products in the same market segment.

Postal surveys Mailing or distributing door-to-door of written questionnaires for potential customers to complete, and perhaps a sample of the product for them to try.

Price The value that the seller attaches to a product or service.

Price competition Price setting in relation to the price charged by competitors; also known as competition-orientated pricing.

Pricing The price structure of a product or range, which takes into consideration its cost, the organisation's objectives, demand, perceived quality, the competition, distribution, legislation and regulations, etc.

Primary sources New data.

Problem children Products which fail to get past their launch stage in the product life cycle.

Product Broadly, anything that is offered to a market that might satisfy a need. A product does not have to be a physical thing – it could be a service or an idea.

Product life cycle A product's beginnings (or launch), growth, maturity and decline in popularity and sales.

Product line A group of products which are closely related, as they are intended for a similar end use, such as Heinz soups.

Product mix The total range of products which an organisation offers.

Profit margins The difference between total costs and selling price of a product or service.

Profitability The successful marrying of a good pricing policy with the costs and market situation, to give a profit to the organisation on sales of the product.

Public Relations (PR) Activities meant to influence favourably the public's perception of an organisation.

Purchasing power Either the disposable income or the discretionary income of the customer.

Questionnaires A series of questions, written or orally delivered, which the respondent is invited to answer.

Research and development (R&D) In an organisation this department is the supposed source of new ideas and suggestions on product innovation, and testing of new products where applicable.

Sales forecasts The process of predicting sales, profits and turnover.

Sales promotion Short-term incentives to encourage purchases.

Sampling Investigating a representative sample of the market.

Scheduling The planning of a media campaign by setting out the details in a timetable format.

Screening The process of reducing a large number of product ideas to a manageably smaller number.

Secondary sources Previously collected data.

Segmentation The process of breaking down markets into groups with some common traits that might usefully be targeted.

Service An intangible activity that is usually a professional skill, such as hairdressing or advertising.

Stars Products which have successfully reached their growth stage.

Targeting The policy of matching the organisation and its products with a market segment or segments that exhibit need for the product.

Telephone surveys Short and to-the-point interviews over the telephone that aim to research into consumer attitudes, opinions and behaviour.

Telesales Selling products by telephone.

Test marketing A limited launch of a product, to test response.

Trademark A symbol, word or picture which is associated with a particular product or a product range, and may be registered to give it legal protection.

USP Unique selling proposition – something which makes the product unique or sufficiently different from other products.

Variable costs Costs which vary with the value of goods made and sold.